GRACEFULLY BROKEN WONDERFULLY RESTORED

Overcoming Spiritual Seduction

Chinnita Morris

1st Fruits Publishing

Unless otherwise stated, Scripture quotes are taken or paraphrased from the Holy Bible, King James Version (KJV), the New International Version (NIV), the New Living Translation (NLT), and the New King James Version (NKJV).

ISBN 978-1-64184-172-6 (paperback)
ISBN 978-1-64184-171-9 (hardcover)

Copyright © 2019 by Chinnita Morris

All rights reserved. No part of this publication may be reproduced, distributed, or transmitted in any form or by any means, including photocopying, recording, or other electronic or mechanical methods without the prior written permission of the publisher. For permission requests, solicit the publisher via the address below.

For booking Chinnita Morris, please contact:
Mari Sanders @ A to Z entertainment Inc.
865.689.7376 DL
Mari@AtoZentinc.com
Chinnitamorris.com

1st Fruits Publishing

Printed in the United States of America

To my sister Tonya and all who are in bondage to anything.

They overcame him by the blood of the Lamb and by the word of their testimony, and they loved not their lives, unto death.

—Revelation 12:11 KJV

See the devil, he learns from your mistakes, even if you don't... that's how he keeps you in cycles.

—Jonathan McReynolds

Contents

Foreword by Pastor Daryl Arnold 11
Preface 13
Acknowledgments 15
Introduction 19

Chapter 1: Mountain Top 23
Chapter 2: Kingdom Connections 33
Chapter 3: So We Meet Again 42
Chapter 4: New Friends but Who Sent You? 51
Chapter 5: There's More To It 58
Chapter 6: Something in My Spirit Ain't Right 67
Chapter 7: James 1:20 - Human Anger Doesn't Produce
    God's Righteousness 75
Chapter 8: Wait... What Just Happened? 84
Chapter 9: Seduced 90
Chapter 10: Transparent 94
Chapter 11: The Fight of My Life 102
Chapter 12: I Do What I Hate 110
Chapter 13: The Longer You Stay 114
Chapter 14: Broken and Contrite 129

Chapter 15: My Darkest Hour 140

Chapter 16: The Devil Will Find a Way Back 149

Chapter 17: Out of Egypt 154

Chapter 18: A Thorn in My Flesh 158

Chapter 19: Overcoming Strongholds and Spiritual Seduction 167

    Part One: How to recover from failure or bondage 167

    Part Two: The responsibility of holding someone
        accountable 174

Chapter 20: Luke 22:32 - Strengthen Your Brothers 177

Foreword

For over fifteen years, our ministry has closed every service with one solitary faith confession. "And they overcame him by the blood of the Lamb, and by the word of their testimony; and they loved not their lives unto the death" (Revelation 12:11).

Most Believers understand the importance of the Blood of the Lamb, but we don't think that it is equally important to share the Word of our testimony. James 5 says that we should confess our faults one to another that we may be healed. The reason so many Christian are saved but not healed is because they have not yet developed the courage to confess their faults. This book will teach you how to allow the grace and mercy of God to heal you everywhere you hurt.

Chinnitta Morris has used her own personal experiences of struggling with silent sin, which was leading her into a pit of condemnation as a testimony of how God can redeem, reconcile, and even recover all that you have lost if you ultimately fully turn to Him. This is a transparent story of a woman that was blessed by *God,* broken by *guilt,* yet rebuilt by *grace*.

If you or anyone that you love feels stuck in their sin, their circumstances or a seemly unbreakable stronghold, this book will definitely help break the chains.

Pastor Daryl W. Arnold
Overcoming Believers Church
Knoxville, Tennessee

Preface

Chinnita Morris entered the year 2006 on a mountain high. The year before had its struggles but ended with great accomplishments and milestones for Chinnita. God had shown Himself strong in areas she had only dreamed of. After committing her life to Christ in 1998 while thriving in the secular entertainment industry, Chinnita had struggled to be accepted and find her place in the Gospel industry and ministry. But after being licensed to minister, consistent comedy events and tours and getting an invite to minister through comedy at one of her favorite gospel artist's conference, things seemed to be turning in her favor.

Regardless of struggling to be accepted by the church who had witnessed her worldly style of comedy on TV programs such as *Def Comedy Jams* and B.E.T.'s *ComicView*, when Chinnita Morris (a.k.a. Chocolate) committed her life to Christ, she was fully committed, and in spite of how hard things got, she wasn't going back. Chinnita's love for her Lord and Savior was obvious to all who were ever in her company or had the privilege to carry on a conversation with her. Clearly, she had found the love of her life in Jesus Christ and her heart's desire was to live a life that please Him and bring Him great honor and glory. Nothing else in life mattered more to her. Walking in victory, she was on a mountain high.

So imagine how she must have felt to find herself in the year 2006 in the fight of her life to overcome the sin she was knee deep in, with no desire to be there.

Gracefully Broken is a true story about Chinnita's experience to overcome a sin she had no desire to be in but had to fight daily to get out of. A sin that was out to destroy her life, her ministry, and her testimony.

Broken and ashamed, but not destroyed, God would take this experience to show Chinnita the sins of her heart and what had to change as she continued to walk with Him. God had already strategically placed two people in her life who would walk with her through this horrific experience and teach her His heart through them.

Little did Chinnita know when she came into the year 2006, it would be a year she would cry more tears than she ever had before, become more broken and humbled than she ever imagined and experience more grace than she ever imagined she would need. In 2006, God allowed Chinnita to be gracefully broken and wonderfully restored.

Acknowledgments

First and foremost to my amazingly wonderful and incredible Redeemer, my Savior and Lord Jesus Christ, you keep me in awe of your faithfulness, your loving-kindness, your patience, and your unfailing love toward me. Mere words cannot express my gratitude for your great and *amazing grace* in my life. I love you, Father, more than I can ever express, but that won't stop me from trying. Thank you, Father so much for the love you show me through your chastening. I do not despise your correction, Lord, for I desire to live according to your will that you would be glorified. Thank you for saving me and raising me to a higher standard of living. When I was living deep in sin and ignorance to your will for my life, you came and rescued me. When I look back over my life, I realize that you have always been there fighting my battles when the enemy was trying to take me out. I can never thank you enough, Father. I was able to walk out of this very situation victorious because you never left me for a moment. You were with me every step of the way. Thank You for your faithfulness to me even when I am unfaithful to you, Lord. I am eternally grateful for all that you have already done and that which you are going to do in my life. I am in absolute awe of you, Father. My heart is yours; my life belongs to you. I surrender all, Father. Have your way. I'm overwhelmed by your goodness and mercy and grace. Thank you for teaching me what true love looks like.

To my beloved mother, Saundra Shoats Carethers, I am your legacy—the good, the bad, and the ugly. This is the one thing I never had the heart to share with you. I couldn't bear to break your heart with such failure. I loved you too much to do that to you, and I knew that God would bring me out. Our relationship and your redemption story is a testament to me that God is more than able to restore everything the enemy took from us. Thank you for believing in me and being my biggest fan from my brokest days to my wealthiest days. In spite of all we went through, I wouldn't trade you for nothing! I am so proud of you, and I will always honor you, Momma. I am grateful to God to be called one of San's six girls. We miss you, beloved. Rest in the arms of your Savior. I will see you when I get there.

Mr. James "Fuzzy" Ferguson (director of Recreation at Erwin Youth Center, Gastonia, North Carolina). I believe in giving honor where honor is due. Sir, you were the one God used to change the trajectory of my life. You watched me grow up at the youth center. And when it was time to graduate high school, you knew my circumstances and asked me what my plans were. I didn't think I was smart enough for college, and I certainly didn't have the money to go, so I didn't even try to apply for college or even take the SAT. I had decided to go to the Air Force. You asked me to give you permission to send someone to speak to me about college before I made that decision and if you could get me in, would I go. I told you I didn't have money for that. You told me you would work on all that, and you did. You got me accepted in to college on a Pell Grant. I would go on to graduate from WSSU. Going to college changed my outlook on life completely. I realized I could do anything I put my mind to. And I have you to thank for that, sir. I know that you helped so many of us overcome our situations to go on and have a better life than what we came from. And I'm not sure if I've ever formally thanked you. But I can't thank you enough, Mr. Ferguson, and I will always be grateful to God for you, sir. I pray to honor you by paying it forward. May you rest in eternal peace. I will never forget your unselfish labor of love.

To my daughter, Imani Symone, and my grandson, Christian Josiah, you are what God has used to show me glimpses of heaven. I love you more than you will ever know. You bring my heart so much joy, and I praise God for blessing me with you both. You are my greatest inspirations. And I'm believing God to raise a holy nation through you both. You are my legacy.

To Pastor Daryl Arnold, where do I begin but at the beginning on that fateful night when I was booked for the Valentine's Day event at your church. I didn't realize that night that it was a divine connection, but you did. You actually said it that night! I am lost for words to describe how God has used you to grow me in my walk with Him. Thank you for loving me like Jesus through my darkest hour. I can't imagine what I would've done without someone to believe that I didn't want to be where I was. Thank you for your patience with me and for not giving up on me. I honor your wife, Carmisha, for the awesome woman of God that she is. I look at her and see the heart I am supposed to have as a wife, and I am encouraged. I love and thank God for you both.

To Minister Demetrus Stewart, I had only known you for a short period of time before all this happened, but I believe it was God's divine design for us to connect because He would use you and your incredible prayer life to get me through such a horrific experience. Thank you so much for understanding my plight and for availing yourself to hold me accountable. Thank you for praying for me. You are a prayer warrior, and I believe that when you pray, heaven rejoices to hear your voice and delights to respond to your request. I am grateful to God for you, my friend.

To my sisters Bev, Lisa, Tonya, Marva, and Allis, thank you for being my sisters, my headache, my help, my encourager, my inspiration, my sparring partners, my forgiving siblings. Sorry you guys had to find out like this, but as Momma would say, you know you can't hold water! I love you guys more than you will ever know. And I'm grateful to God for us. #Sanslegacy.

To Jennifer, April and James, Chinita, Sharonda, Jasmine, Adakalon, Jaqi, Lisa, and everyone I love and those who love me in spite of me, thank you. I'm blessed to have you in my life. I love you all. Lisa Mills, Jaqi Wright, and Pastor Daryl Arnold, I want to especially thank you for laboring in prayer for me while I wrote this book. You know it took a lot out of me, but your prayers kept me going. I'm grateful to you all for that. May the Lord bless you richly in your every godly endeavor. Thank you so much! I love you all! God bless.

Introduction

It's been exactly twelve years this year, and it still makes me emotional to think about it all. I've started and stopped a few times not knowing which direction to go with it or how to convey my story with integrity without saying too much to where it's offensive, or saying too little and compromise the integrity of the story.

My heart is beating fast just knowing all that this book will require of me. But I remember reading the book *God Chasers* by Tommy Tenny a long time ago, and he said something that really blessed me. I'm paraphrasing, but basically, he said, "If you want to see the church catch on fire for God, throw yourself on the altar."

Personally, I believe God keeps bringing that to my remembrance for a reason. And I get it. You will too once you hear my story. So I solicit your patience as I try to tell this story with the help of the Holy Spirit. It wasn't an easy one to get out. But here it goes!

See, I've been meaning to and wanting to write this book for years knowing that I was called to do it. But a thousand and one distractions hindered me, as well as this thing called life. And not to mention my lack of discipline.

The enemy has been determined to keep me from sharing my story because he knows it's going to mess up his plans to steal, kill, and destroy many who will read this book and share its message.

As people of God, our heart's desire should be to love everyone as Christ loves them. As a matter of fact, that was the one new commandment He gave—that we love each other as He has loved us... and that by this men will know that we are His disciples (John 13:34).

God said He would have it that no man would perish but that all should come to repentance (2 Peter 3:8). And we should feel the same way about people, so much so that we are willing to present our bodies as a living sacrifice and share not just the glamourous testimonies but the good, the bad, and the ugly, embarrassing ones too!

The ones that speak to others that may be in similar situations to let them know that they are not alone. You are not the only one who has experienced this horrible failure.

We have to learn to take off the mask and let people know that we mess up too. Sometimes, horribly! But that with God's grace and mercy, we got through it, and so can they.

I believe that one of the biggest problems with the church today is we all want to walk around like we've got it all together. Nobody wants to show their scars. Many of us are so full of pride that we can be in situations we know we can't get out of on our own yet we refuse to ask for help. Afraid of people seeing our dirt, our hurt, or knowing our weaknesses.

Then many of us are too prideful to allow others to hold us accountable. And then others don't have the courage or the "time" to hold someone accountable.

Then it's hard to share your failures with people in the church because you can barely trust anyone to keep it between you, them, and God. But here's a hint, if you've heard that person freely sharing information about other people that they shouldn't be sharing (gossiping), that's probably not someone you want to confide in.

I personally don't want people in my life (close circle) who are too afraid to hold me accountable if you see me in sin. And I don't really care for you to be in my circle if you have a problem being held accountable if I see you've fallen into sin. To me, that's the definition of a true brother or sister in Christ, and that's what real love does. I've known people to not address someone's sin because they didn't want to lose the friendship. If you care more about our friendship than you care about my Salvation, then you've misconstrued the whole message of Christ.

I guess the point I'm trying to make is that we be mature Christian's showing the love that God has called us to in His Word so that those who are broken can have someone they can trust with their failures. Too often, the church has been known for killing their wounded. Hence, the reason so many walk around in pain, hurting, and confused with no one to turn to, afraid of being put on the cross and crucified like our Savior who's already paid for our sins once and for all. Don't get me wrong. I'm not talking about people who are in sin and okay with where they are and spew rhetoric like "Only God can judge me," "God knows my heart," or "It don't take all of that." When you hear people readily defend sin, they pretty much enjoy being in sin. Don't argue with them. They're not ready to surrender. Proverbs 1:7 says the fear of the Lord is the beginning of wisdom, but fools despise wisdom and instruction.

This book is a reflection of the author's recollection of the events that took place. Most of the names have been changed to protect the privacy of the innocent participants.

Chapter 1
Mountain Top

In late August or early September 2005, I received a call asking if I could do comedy for an all-girls conference in October for Gospel artist Neicy Wray. WHAAAAATTT! Neicy Wray! OMGness!!! It was all I could do to keep my composure. I could not let her know how overjoyed I was to be getting this call—that would be so unprofessional. But I admired her and her stand for holiness, and to hear that I was being called on to be a part of something she was doing was just pure joy to my spirit. I praised God for the opportunity. I admired Neicy for her music and her stand for Christ in the industry. Unfortunately, you can't say that about many in the Gospel industry so it is refreshing to meet those who do stand up for holiness and righteousness and not bow down to the "idol god entertainment industry."

But she used her God-given gifts and platform to lift up the name of Jesus Christ that lost souls would come to Christ.

Now I said all that to let you know what getting a call to do this event meant to me.

My only concern was doing a show for young girls. I do women's conferences all the time, and my material is perfect for grown women because I talk about grown woman stuff. LOL! Not sure the young girls will get it. But she assured me it would be fine.

So now we were negotiating my honorarium. And we quickly agreed on what I would get paid to perform. What she didn't know was that I would've done it for free because it was a blessing to finally get to work with Neicy Wray because she was a great inspiration to me in my walk with God.

But I wasn't turning down no money because Christian comedy has had me struggling for a minute now. But that's another book. LOL!

Plus, what she was doing was a beautiful idea for girls and young women, ages thirteen to thirty, teaching them godly principles and self-worth, ministering and preaching the Gospel to them. She also had other great Gospel artists on this two-day event that would start on Friday evening and end on Saturday evening, and worship service at Neicy's church home on Sunday morning would be the culmination of the whole event.

By this time, I had been doing comedy for fifteen years. Seven of those years had now been as a Christian comedian. I had toured with and opened for some of the greatest in the entertainment industry, secular and Gospel. But for me, this event would be the icing on the cake. I felt like this was God's favor on me. I was overjoyed that God would see fit to bless and allow me this privilege when were so many other Christian comedians who could have been chosen. But God chose me. All glory to God. So I definitely wanted to make my Father proud and be a blessing to Neicy's conference.

The time finally came for the conference in October 2005 in Nashville, Tennessee. I took my ten-year-old daughter with me because she loved a few of the other Gospel artists who would be on the event as well. She was ecstatic about accompanying me on this event, which was not always the case. She only likes to go if there are Gospel artists on the event that she likes to listen to. And she loved the singing sisters. She had actually met them before at a Gospel artists' retreat in Las Vegas a couple of years prior to this event.

So we got to Nashville early that day and chilled out in our hotel room before the first night's event kicked off. Man, was I nervous! Certain people you just don't want to let down when God gives you that platform!

Neicy would call all the artists down to meet her in the greenroom about an hour before the event would start. She wanted to make sure she went over the event schedule with us and some other preliminaries for the show.

We all sat around the green room waiting for Neicy to get there and then the singing sisters walked in. They greeted us with hugs, and my daughter was so happy to see them again. They began to make themselves some tea and were a bit comical with their banter back and forth with each other. We all chuckled at their antics.

Then Neicy walked in and flashed her beautiful smile as she hugged and greeted everybody. When she saw my daughter Imani, she bent down and gave her a big hug and asked her whose beautiful daughter she was. She chatted with my daughter for a moment, and Mani was smiling from ear to ear loving every minute of it. This was her first time ever meeting Mrs. Neicy Wray in person, although she was very much aware of who she was.

Then Neicy got real serious real quick and called us all to gather around because she wanted to go over some formalities. She began to go over the dress code and told the singing sisters they were going to have to pin up their blouses because her mother was there and "y'all know she don't play that." We all laughed about it as they commenced to pinning up their blouses. Because we couldn't show any cleavage, which was easy for me because I don't have a "big" problem in that area. Pun intended. But I will say that they were very upfront about our dress code in a package that they sent out about a month before the event, telling us all to be mindful of our attire because we would be ministering to very influential young ladies. But now I was really nervous because her mother was here too! Much respect for that woman of God!

So the event began at 6:00 p.m. and went on like clockwork. Neicy went out and was the first to greet all the young ladies. The house was jam-packed! The conference was to accommodate five hundred girls, but the response for such a conference was so overwhelming they had to make room for two hundred more. These young ladies came from all over the United States and all nationalities under one roof, celebrating Christ and learning how to be more like Him. It was *awesome*!

Neicy brought the singing sisters up first. (Really, Neicy, you got me going on after the singing sisters!) They ripped the stage (means they did incredibly well). I could tell my daughter was enjoying them because she was singing every song to the top of her lungs. Everybody was jamming to the music. The singing sisters brought the house down.

And now it was my turn and I think I was more nervous than I had ever been. It is always my desire that God be glorified through my ministry. But the added pressure was this was Neicy Wray and her mom was here! And although I do "Christian comedy," would it be Christian enough for them? And I know some of y'all are probably saying, "Don't put them on a pedestal. If it's good enough for God, it should be good enough for them." But listen, her parents have managed to do what the many Christians miss the mark on, and that's raising up a Holy Nation in the earth (1 Peter 2:9).

"But they are human and they fall short just like anybody else," you say. Which is what drives my point home. That they are just as human as any of us, and in their humanity, they decided they would deny their flesh and the opinions of many who would criticize them for being too strict on their children, because their way was unorthodox compared to the world's way. But it was the way God had called them to. And God honored their sacrifices as they raised up a holy nation unto Him. And there is no refuting that. So I'm not saying they're perfect, and I'm not putting them on a pedestal. Just giving honor where honor is due.

Because Godly people inspire me to be a better Christian and I hope to do the same for others. When you see people overcome the things of the world and make sacrifices to live holy in spite of what everyone else is doing, then that lets you know it can be done. And that's why we are called to be walking epistles of Christ (2 Corinthians 3:2–3).

So now I'm shaking in my black canvas pumps because the house is packed and singing sisters just wrecked the stage and Neicy is about to introduce me. Yikes! I began to pray as I always do before going onstage, "Lord, use me as you please. Let my gift of comedy bring great laughter that restores the joy that has been lost and bring healing to those who are hurting and need to hear from You, Father. You are the lifter of our heads. Have your way, Holy God. I surrender all. In Jesus's name I pray, Amen."

And have His way He did. I had so much fun on that stage that I ran out of time and had to cut it short so as to not go over my time. When I got off stage, even the singing sisters were clowning me and was still laughing about things I had said. Then they were about to leave to go get something to eat but told me they had to see my performance first. Praise God! I was so relieved to be done with my part of the event. Now I could relax and enjoy the rest of the conference. Thank you, Jesus!

The event would continue to escalate that night until it was finally over. Other great Gospel artists as well as Neicy would go on to close out the event. And I dare to say that I'm sure there were no regrets for anyone who made the sacrifice to be there. There was a heavy anointing and presence of God in that room with us all.

The first night would end with a meet and greet, autograph signing, and picture taking, and all the artists had to participate. Afterward, as hungry as we were, Mani and I were more tired than anything and decided to just go to our room famished but too tired to eat. So we just went to bed because tomorrow's events would start in the early afternoon and end early evening.

The next day, my daughter and I got up early to get ready to go downstairs because Neicy had scheduled for all the artist to have brunch with her and her mother before the second half of the conference began. Brunch was great, or maybe it was just because Mani and I was so hungry from the night before. But the fellowship was even better. The best part for me was talking to Neicy's mother. But I could tell that my ten-year-old daughter now had a new favorite Gospel artist. She was enjoying chatting it up with Neicy.

The young ladies were excited and eager for the second half to start. The headliner was coming on soon. But before he would take the stage, the lady I had met in the greenroom the day before in the white Kangol hat would be ministering. Not many people knew who she was before she ministered, but after she was done, none of us would ever forget her. She shared her powerful testimony of her life's journey, trials, and tribulations. She was a beautiful woman with an even more beautiful spirit. She ministered with such an anointing that many of the girls were overcome with the Holy Spirit and crying uncontrollably. The presence of the Lord was heavy in the room. My daughter was even overcome with emotion as she held on to my waist, and I held her tightly as I began weeping as well.

This went on for some time, and when the room was finally brought to order, Minister Claudia began to minister as the Spirit of God led her to.

I remember her speaking directly to me from the stage. She asked her pastor's wife to come over and cover me in prayer. And while she and someone else did so, Minister Claudia began to encourage me from the stage and tell me to not grow weary in my singleness and even admonished me to be mindful of those who would try to come into my life because the enemy knows my situation and my vulnerability and would use it against me. Little did I know, she was speaking prophetically to me that day. I only wish I had remembered this moment when the attack began. It would've made more sense and I would've responded differently. Unfortunately, I forgot. (SN.) Make a note of it anytime someone speaks a prophecy to you.

The power of God was unmistakable that day. It didn't matter what denomination you came with. We were all Pentecostal that day! LOL! It was a great blessing to witness the Spirit of the Most High God move so mightily in the conference that afternoon. We all needed to gather ourselves afterward and pull it together. So she gave us all a thirty-minute break before bringing up the headliner for the conference. During the break, some went for refreshments and some went to regroup from tearing up their makeup and hair. But many of us stood around talking and mingling. I got compliments from a lot of the girls about how hard I had them laughing and how much they enjoyed the comedy show. I signed some autographs and took more pictures.

There were two girls in particular who came up to me during the break to thank me for blessing them to have so much fun on their first night there. They also had a gift for me in a small bag with a card.

The gift was a little stuffed animal, and the card simply said, "See this smile... you put that there." I'll never forget it because it made me laugh. They introduced themselves to me. We chatted briefly, and I was blessed to know that my ministry blessed them. They both gave me and my daughter a hug and then disappeared into the crowd.

I never forgot them because the gesture was so sweet. And even though they introduced themselves to me, I did forget their names.

I've always been horrible at remembering faces and names if we didn't have an extensive conversation or spend significant time together. What I did remember was that one of them was a bit eccentric, with the natural afro pulled back by a head wrap and kind of seventies clothing, and the other one didn't talk as much as the eccentric one. But they both seemed to be enjoying the conference.

Once the break was over, we all went back into the room the conference was being held, and now it was time for the headliner to minister. As he took the stage, he sat on a stool and many of the girls began to scream for him. So much so that Neicy had to get on the mic and tell them to calm down and to let them know that their behavior was inappropriate because, first of all, he was a married man and we were Christians.

Once they got their feelings in check, he really had a heart to heart with those young ladies and said things to them that they needed to hear from a man's perspective. It even blessed me and gave me insight and I was thirty-nine years old at the time. LOL! He spoke candidly to them about being godly women and carrying themselves in ways that would attract godly men.

The headliner did a magnificent job of telling the girls things that they needed to hear from a fatherly perspective on loving and respecting themselves first to receive the love and respect they deserve as children of God.

As much as we were being fed the Word of God through many of His different vessels, I think it's safe to say this is an event no one wanted to end. At least not yet. I think the only thing many of us were disappointed in was the fact that it was only two days. Everyone left wanting more. I had done many conferences, but thus far, this one surpassed them all. All the girls were given Bibles and tiaras and told they were priceless princesses.

My daughter had the time of her life! And now although she still loved the singing sisters, Neicy Wray had taken their spot and they had been moved down a notch. I'm just grateful the girl loves Gospel music.

After the event ended that day around 5:00 or 6:00 p.m., it was still pretty early and most people stood around talking and taking pictures with the artist that were still there.

This also turned out to be an event where many of the girls who were meeting each other for the first time would become friends for a lifetime.

Even Mani and I made friends while there that would become like sisters to us—Allison and her daughter Kacey. I was about three years older than Allison and Mani was two years younger than Kacey. We all met the first night of the conference, but we didn't exchange e-mails until the next day after taking pictures together and talking for a while. Allison and her daughter thought it was hilarious how Mani was standing on the chair the first night singing the singing sisters' songs to the top of her lungs.

Although Kacey was two years older than Imani, she was short so they were about the same height. Allison and her daughter were pretty short in stature and they looked like twins. It was the cutest thing. So we hit it off and vowed to keep in touch after the conference.

After a while, the crowd dwindled down, and people had left either to go get something to eat or just went back to their rooms.

Mani and I were hungry and tired so our assigned adjutant (can't remember her name) for the weekend took us out to eat, and afterward, she brought us back to the hotel to get some rest because, again, in the morning, we would have to be up early for church, even though we were only going to the second service. This would be the culmination of the whole conference.

The next morning, Mani and I had to be packed and dressed for church because we would not be coming back to the hotel. While getting dressed, to my surprise I realized that I had made the mistake of packing the wrong shoes for church, and they didn't match my dress suit. (SN.) I pretty much dressed like a missionary for church during that time in my walk with Christ. LOL! And to my dismay, I had to wear the black pumps that I wore onstage at the conference. I felt really tacky. That morning was really cold, as was the whole weekend. It was October in Nashville, so it was no surprise. And Minister Claudia was picking us up for church. When we got in the car, she explained that Neicy Wray would not be attending worship service with us because she had another event she had to be at. I could see Imani's obvious disappointment, but she quickly got over it.

I also commenced to explaining why my shoes didn't match my dress with a bit of embarrassment might I add. She assured me I looked fine as we drove off. That wasn't really comforting to hear but I didn't protest. Furthermore, I wasn't sure I could rely on her word since she looked a bit "missionary-ish" herself. Funny thing is, had I had on the shoes I intended to bring, we would've been almost dressed alike! LOL!

Worship service was great! I love churches that have a spirit of excellence within. Not doing things just for the sake of doing it but truly following God's lead. Most of the girls from the conference went to the first service. I think Neicy went to that one as well. There were still quite a few of the girls from the conference at the second service. Some went to both services. I enjoyed service so much that I inquired about the sister church they have in the Atlanta area since I was in the market for a new church home.

We were greeted by a lot of the girls from the conference, and then we ran into Allison and Kacey as this was their church home too. We all hugged and greeted one another and had a few laughs and again vowed to keep in touch before departing ways. After leaving church, Minister Claudia took us out to dinner. It was a long drive but well worth it once we got there. One of her friends from church met us there as well. The food and fellowship was great. Minister Claudia had a beautiful smile and an even more beautiful, kind, and humble spirit. She made you feel like you've been friends forever. She was a jewel, a rare pearl. Little did I know at the time that I would come to know this as an undeniable fact.

Once we were done with dinner, she took Imani and me to the airport where we would say our goodbyes and express our gratitude for inviting us to be a part of this phenomenal conference. One we will never forget... for more reasons than we know of right now.

Mani asked Minister Claudia to tell Neicy she said bye, and she promised she would.

An event like this for young girls was very necessary and long overdue, and I was glad to be invited to be a part of it. So many of those girls came there hurting, lost, lonely, and trying to figure out life and love and how to walk this walk according to God's will in the society we live in today. It's hard for most adults, so I can only imagine how so many of them must feel. But the ministries that went forth spoke to every situation. No one should've left the same as they came if they were receptive to what thus saith the Lord.

Many of us met people who would touch our lives in ways that would leave an indelible mark for the rest of our lives. Some good and some bad. Unfortunately, some of the connections would end in heartbreak and heartache in ways we would never imagine.

Unfortunately.

Chapter 2
Kingdom Connections

The conference was over, and Mani and I were back home. She was still on cloud nine from the weekend's events and especially meeting Neicy Wray. That was the highlight of the weekend for her, which was funny because I took her because I knew she loved singing sisters. The agent who booked me for the event had sent a package before we went that had a lot of information about the event and also included Neicy Wray's live-in-concert DVD. When we got back home, Mani must have watched that DVD a thousand times. Hilarious!

Now it was time to wind down and ready ourselves for bed because she had school tomorrow. I was exhausted and couldn't wait to get some sleep in my own bed. The hotel was really nice but there is nothing like home for me.

We got up early as usual to get Mani ready for school only today she was so excited to get to school to tell her friends about her weekend. I took Mani and her friends to the bus stop as I normally did each morning. But I was still very tired from the weekend. Thank God the bus stop is only at the top of the subdivision. The kids always waited in the car with me whenever it was cold outside, and it was cold. So Mani couldn't help boast a little about her weekend and the fun she had. Unfortunately, her friends didn't have a clue who the artist were that she spoke of. But they listened anyway and seemed to be excited for her. Finally, the bus pulled up and the boys ran and got on, but I hugged and kissed my baby before she ran to the bus. The only thing I wanted to do when I got back to the house was go to sleep.

As soon as I got home, I went upstairs, and instead of going to my room, I decided to sleep in the guest room, my throne room. This was my prayer room. This room was especially set aside for time with my Father. I had a prayer closet in my bedroom, but this room was consecrated. However, occasionally, I would go in there to rest or for a change of scenery from my own bedroom.

Once I got in the bed, I fell off into a deep sleep, oblivious to everything around me. I was exhausted, so I was sleeping hard. Apparently, I had been sleeping for a few hours before I was abruptly startled by a loud ringing. I heard it but was too out of it to process where it was coming from. Struggling to open my eyes and half-awake, I now realize it's my phone ringing. Not my cell phone but my house phone. (It was 2005, house phones were still very much used.) I checked the caller ID, and all I could see the area code but I didn't have a clue who it could be. I then realized it was a Nashville number, but I know I didn't give anyone that I met my number. I only exchanged e-mail addresses with them. I began to wonder if maybe we left something at the hotel and they were calling to inform us. Then my vision went from blurry to focused, and I could see the whole name. It took a second more to register in my mind... Oh my goodness! *That's* Neicy Wray!

I tried to gather myself so that I wouldn't sound like she just woke me up at eleven thirty in the morning. But in spite of my efforts, I knew it was inevitable. I answered the phone and she asked to speak to me. I said, "Speaking." She greeted me with a great "good morning" like she had been up since before the break of dawn and had done more before 6:00 a.m. than I was going to do all week! She was wide-awake! Trying to sound already woke, I responded "Good morning" back to her. At the same time, I was really taken aback that she was calling me. Oh lawd, did I do something wrong? Lord, help me brace myself for this lashing!

I sat up in the bed trying desperately not to sound like I just woke up, but to no avail. (I felt so trifling.) I'm sure she noticed I was asleep. I probably sounded like Louie Armstrong singing "What a Wonderful World." I wanted to explain myself to let her know that I'm not normally this trifling but I was really tired from the weekend.

But she was the host so if anyone should've been tired, it should be her. So wisdom said, "Just spare her the explanation. You already look stupid."

She started the conversation by letting me know that she was calling to make sure we got home safely and that she hoped we enjoyed ourselves. I told her that our trip was very comfortable and that we thoroughly enjoyed ourselves. I told her how much fun my daughter had and how much I appreciated her having us there and that I hoped she was okay with my comedy. She laughed and told me it was great and that she was a bit concerned in the beginning but that she really enjoyed it. At that point, I wanted to ask her what I did in the beginning that had her concerned. But I decided to take it for what it was and leave it at that. We didn't talk long because I think she sensed that she woke me up. But she was the sweet, jovial, humble Neicy that she always seems to be. She told me to hug and kiss Imani for her and tell her she asked about her before we hung up. I told her I definitely would.

I hung up the phone and thought, *Wow! This woman truly lets the glory of God radiate through her like a thousand watt halogen lamp!* I was so honored that the woman of God took the time to dial my number to thank me for my contribution to the conference and to make sure we were safe at home. She even remembered my daughter's name! Now please don't think I'm tripping because I honestly don't stargaze. Celebrity really doesn't mean much to me. I respect your talent and your grind. But what I respect most is your anointing. I only act like this if you inspire me. I was in awe of her humility and spirit of excellence, going above and beyond to be a blessing. Those are the kinds of Christians I want to sharpen me.

At this point, I was really grateful to God for blessing me with this experience in its entirety. A couple of months later, I would find myself asking why He blessed me to go there.

Later that day, when checking my e-mail, I saw that I had gotten some from many of the girls that I'd met at the conference. What a wonderful surprise. I don't think I was expecting that so soon. I was especially happy to see the e-mail from Allison, the young lady with the daughter who looked just like her. When I read the e-mail, she was trying to make me remember who she was and describing her and her daughter. But trust me, I had not forgotten them at all. She need not go into all of that because I knew exactly who she was. And I was glad to hear from her. I e-mailed her back immediately.

I had also gotten an e-mail from one of the girls who gave me the gift. Her name was Sheila, although I was still oblivious to who was who between the two. Her e-mail was really sweet, thanking me again for the laughter and reminding me to keep in touch. She also left a number for me to call should I feel led to do so.

I e-mailed her back, thanking her for the gift she and her friend gave me and told her it was a pleasure to meet them both. The next day I received an e-mail from her friend as well. Her name was Chloe. She was thanking me for bringing joy to her heart, saying she really needed the laughter and explaining how much she really enjoyed the conference and how glad she was that she came. I let her know that I was glad she enjoyed herself and to God be all glory.

Allison and I would continue to e-mail each other quite a bit for the next few days until we decided it was time to make a phone call. We would stay on the phone for hours laughing and talking and just really getting to know each other. We had quite a bit in common. We were both saved, divorced, and single moms of one daughter. Our daughters were two years apart and we were three. As an entertainer, I didn't have a day job, and I mostly only worked on weekends. So we would talk all hours of the day because she would call me from work and talk to me while she worked. She worked for a family member so she could get away with it as long as her work was done.

We were excited about our newfound friendship. We made each other laugh, hard! She was just as comical as I was. We were developing a strong sisterhood and friendship. Rarely did we go a day without talking and sharing details of our day.

We even took time to speak to each other's daughters on the phone.

Our daughters even developed a friendship and would call each other every now and then. I would even talk with her mom sometimes because I met her at the conference too, but I didn't know she was Allison's mom at the time. Our friendship blossomed very fast, and I don't think either one of us had a problem with that. It wasn't long before we were making plans for her and her daughter to come to Atlanta to spend a weekend with my daughter and me.

In the meantime, some of the other young ladies I had met at the conference had contacted me as well. (This conference just kept on giving long after it was over.) One in particular was the evangelist. I had given her my card when I met her and her husband after she had ministered and we were on our way to our rooms that night. I was elated to hear from her. She was such a sweet spirit. She and her husband were both very pleasant people and the spirit of God was powerful on them. Her testimony was powerful and what she added to the conference will forever resonate in the ears of those who truly listened. She spoke candidly about how she was now "preaching with AIDS" and had written a book by the same title. She was a no-holds-barred-type preacher. She was passionate about getting her point out about seriously living for Christ and not engaging in sexual activity until you are married. She explained how she was out there messing around and got hooked on drugs and how drugs led to much casual sex and casual sex led to AIDS.

And although she didn't know how much longer she would be with us, she was going to use the time she had left to preach the Gospel of Jesus Christ and share her testimony in hopes that souls would be saved. She wasn't sad or bitter, in spite of her many sick days. Still she wanted to be used mightily by God with the time she had left. And I believe it's safe to say that she absolutely did that and some. She truly availed herself to God, and He used her as she had prayed He would to win lost souls to Christ. So it was an incredible joy to receive a call from her just two days after the conference. I'm feeling exceedingly blessed!

This would be the first of quite a few conversations to come. Nothing like how Allison and I spent time talking. No, this was on a more serious note. We mostly talked about our journeys, where we'd come from, and how we got where we are now. We shared our painful past and our joys of serving Jesus.

She would always ask about my daughter Imani, or "the baby" as she would call her. She always showed such sincere concern for Imani. So much so that it almost made we wonder why she was so concerned for my daughter. But then it was a blessing to know that Mani was always on her heart like that. Maybe it was because she had a daughter too that she was very close to. Her daughter was now grown.

She was also blessed to have a handsome husband who adored her and took great care of her. I was blessed in my spirit to see the way this man loved his wife. They were one of the most beautiful couples I had ever met. We didn't talk every day, not even every week. But when we did, I believe it meant the world to both of us.

We were sisters, now forever connected! And I loved her as such. How could I not. She was a blessing from God. Some days when we would talk, she wasn't feeling well, and it would break my heart to know she was going through so much pain. But it helped to know her husband was right there with her, doing everything he could to make her comfortable. Sometimes she would give him the phone and we would briefly chat and he would tell me how stubborn she was being. And we all would laugh. Through it all, I never heard her complain not one time, only giving God glory in spite of it all. She too was a jewel.

One of the downfalls of the conference for me was once it was over, I went a few weeks without accomplishing much of nothing during my days because I'd met new friends that I was now talking to on the phone. I have to admit, I didn't expect this. I have always met people on the road and become long-lasting friends with many of them. But this was a bit of an influx all at once. So it was a blessing and a bit of a curse too.

I mostly talked to Allison, but the young lady Sheila was calling quite frequently as well.

She was a sweet young lady who seemed to have endured a lot at a young age. I think she was about twenty-three years old. I believe she just wanted someone to talk to and to have someone hear her heart. I've always been pretty relatable to hurting people because I've experienced and overcome so much pain in my own life. Praise God I don't look like or sound like what I've been through. But that's another book (no, seriously it's coming).

So if this young lady wanted to stay in touch with me so that she could have someone to talk to, I didn't have a problem with that. She had some family issues and she just needed to talk and release from time to time. I didn't see any harm in that as long as I was able to avail myself when she needed me. She and the other friend that I met were from a really small town, and they grew up together, and I think Chloe was like the sister she never had. Their relationship was odd. They were close but not really. If you talked to one, you would think they were best friends until you talked to the other and realized they were close but I wouldn't call her my best friend. But they had sincere love and concern for each other.

Sheila had obviously taken to me and probably looked at me like a big sis or maybe even a godmother because she called all the time. Even when she really didn't have anything to talk about. She would sometimes casually talk about her day, or if something was bothering her, she would run it by me as if asking for my advice. I always made time to talk to her as often as I could. She was a bit needy. But it was ok I guess. She wasn't married or even dating but she wanted to be. You could tell she had a lot of love in her heart that she wanted to share and have it reciprocated back to her. She was very loved. She had love all around her but in pockets, and she needed it to be consistent. And if it was, she didn't see it.

Sheila was a good girl. Raised in the church and serving God faithfully and a faithful servant in her church. She had a good heart. She seemed too serious to be so young. When you heard her laugh, it was refreshing because it was rare coming from her. I couldn't tell whether she was enjoying life or just living. And I didn't have much to offer but genuine kindness and love. But if me being a part of her life brought her just a little joy, just to know she could call and talk to me, then it was worth the time it took to talk to her.

But talking to Sheila was nothing like talking to Allison. With Allison, there was never a dull moment, and I so looked forward to talking to her daily. She was just a lot of fun. Even our serious conversations turned silly. Sometimes we acted like silly little girls laughing till we cried. I guess we both needed it. We had both endured some pain going through our recent divorces, and of course, being single mothers is a task in itself.

However, sometimes when Sheila called, she was just calling. No real reason. And it was obvious because the conversation was dry and dragging and struggling to have a point. But I felt like I needed to be there on the phone with her if she needed me to. She didn't seem suicidal or anything, just needed to be noticed, loved, given some attention just because. I guess in a way, I feel like God was saying they were looking for Him, and He's saying, "Show them Me." And honestly, it's not always easy, especially in those moments when you don't feel like being bothered. And yes, I have those moments, more often than people think because I'm a bit of an introvert. LOL!

But because of my profession, I have to press past it. I really didn't learn how to until I gave my life to Christ and realized my life was not my own, and that in this walk, sacrifice was necessary. You don't always get to do things the way you want to anymore. But we surrender our will to God daily.

Now fast-forward a couple of months, Allison and I had become really, really good friends. She and her daughter had come down to visit us in December right before the Christmas holidays. We all had a blast together.

Sheila and I had a pretty cool friendship by this time as well. She confided in me a lot and just talked about life in general. Where she was now and her plans for her future. She really wanted to leave her small hometown, but she was faithful to serving at her church home. I think it gave her a sense of purpose and made her feel needed. But it kept her around people who were much older than her, and at twenty-three, we all know that can be a drag!

Her friend Chloe was living in Jacksonville, Florida, for the past few years. But whenever she came home to visit, Sheila would be right there at her parents' house with her.

Well, now the Christmas holidays were over and we were on the edge of beginning a new year in less than a week and I had a few end-of-the-year engagements.

Sheila heard about the one in Gainesville, Florida, and wanted to come since it was not a far drive from her. She and Chloe decided to meet up and drive down together. I informed them that I wouldn't be able to hang out with them much because I had to leave early the next morning to fly out to get to my next engagement. They said they didn't mind and that they really wanted to make a girls' trip out of it. I thought it would be great to see them again. Although by this time, I can't remember what either one of them look like.

Chapter 3
So We Meet Again

They called when they got to the venue and I had left tickets for them up front and had instructed for them to be brought to my dressing room. When they arrived, as happy as I was to see them again, I didn't have a clue which one was Chloe and which was Sheila, even though I talked to Sheila many, many times since the conference. I guess because they're from the same place their accents were the same and so I couldn't go on voice. They sounded just alike. I felt terrible not knowing who was who and I didn't dare let on that I didn't know for fear of my own embarrassment and disappointing a fragile Sheila who had spent so much time with me on the phone over the past two months. So during conversations, I stayed away from addressing them by name on purpose. Hoping one would say the other's name and I could figure it out from there. But that didn't happen. Ugh!

One had an afro and a pretty smile and was really skinny and had on these really high heels. I was baffled as to why she would wear such high heels not knowing how far she would have to walk to the venue. (That wasn't wisdom.) Though that may have been her norm, she didn't look comfortable in them. It was painful to watch. They both wore glasses and was about the same height.

So we chopped it up in the dressing room for a bit and got to know each other a little more. Funny thing is because I didn't know who was who, I wasn't sure which one I knew better from phone conversations. This was hilarious! But I didn't want to give myself away and admit that I didn't know. If it had just been to save my face, I would've but I really didn't want to hurt Sheila's feelings.

I took them around to meet some of the other comedians, and they were really excited about one of them who was a really young comedian and was doing well in the industry, and they thought he was the cutest thing.

Right before the event started, they went out to go sit in the audience to watch the show. It wasn't a big turnout, and but the show went on, and the audience came ready to laugh and have a great time and so we did. It was a great show.

After the show, the limo took all the comedians back to the hotel, and Chloe and Sheila followed the limo to the hotel. At this time, we were hungry and just wanted to get something to eat. But because it was late and I had to be up early to catch my flight, I thought it would be best to just order a pizza. They agreed. So that's what we did.

While waiting on our pizza, some of the comedians were coming down the hall being loud and rowdy and decided to stop by my room. The girls were delighted to be in their company especially the young comedian. He really had them excited. They were smiling from ear to ear. They wanted to take pictures with him, and he had no problem obliging them. After a while, they left, and it got quiet in the room again.

It was late, and instead of driving back that night, we agreed it would be best if they just stayed in my room and leave in the morning, which was fine even though I only had a king-size bed. And because of my event the next day, I would have to leave Gainesville at 5:30 a.m.

And even though I didn't know much about them, I trusted them to leave the room intact when they left the next morning.

We all stayed up pretty late talking and laughing. I still didn't know who was who, and I got tired of the facade, so I just decided to ask. They both fell out laughing, especially Chloe, who seemed quite giddy all night. I really should've known from her jovial spirit because Sheila was rarely jovial on the phone. But I don't think I was paying attention to those things.

Even though she laughed along with Chloe, Sheila did seem to be a bit offended that I didn't know which one she was, considering the fact that we had talked so much on the phone and all she had shared with me. I was extremely apologetic, but in my defense, they sounded so much alike. I really should've just ask when they first arrived.

Well, now that that was out of the way, I decided to get in the shower while we wait for the pizza to get there. So I left the money for the pizza with them in case they came while I was in the shower. They did. I was fully dressed in my pajamas when I came out of the bathroom to find the pizza there hot and ready to eat. As we ate, we talked and Chloe began to look through my Bible as she lay across the bed and laughed about how well read it was. (I mark and write in my Bible a lot.) She was quite observant as she also commented on how much she liked these pink suede boots I had brought with me but didn't wear because it was hot. I told her she could have them if she could wear them (and I meant it), but she couldn't. They were a half size too small.

Allison had called while we were eating pizza. She knew they were driving down to meet me for the show. We talked for a minute and she told me to tell them hello. And as usual, she and I began to act silly on the phone. The girls must have thought we were some silly adults. But Chloe chimed right in with us and joined the fun.

While Sheila had made herself comfortable on the little couch and was dozing off, Chloe and I was going through my Bible when all of a sudden this horrible smell took over the room. Chloe and I looked at each other with our faces tore up, like, "did you do that?" Once we realized neither one of us did it, we turned to Sheila whose eyes were closed as if she were asleep but then she confessed it was her before we could even ask. She apologized and said it was the cheese from the pizza. We all got a good laugh from it.

It was now about 2:00 a.m., and we were all winding down, full and sleepy. Sheila said she was comfortable where she was on the couch, and I gave her the extra cover from the closet. Chloe and I shared the bed, while she slept way on one side and I slept way on the other. It's a wonder one of us didn't fall off the bed.

My alarm went off at 5:00 a.m. I didn't hesitate to get up, but I moved around with caution and very little light so as not to wake them. I got dressed and gathered my things to leave. I wanted to leave a note, but it's dark, my hands were full, and I really got to go. I didn't want to wake them this early, but I didn't want to leave without saying goodbye, so I just softly kissed them both on the forehead. It didn't wake them and I was glad. I wanted them to know I had a great time with them and was glad they came.

As I reached the hotel lobby, I saw the limo outside and the driver waiting inside to take me to the airport. It was still very dark out, so on the way to the airport, I took the liberty to get a little more sleep since I only had less than three hours of sleep.

I got back to Atlanta around 8:00 a.m. When I got home, my sitter Tia left shortly after we talked a bit. Then I lay down to get more sleep before getting on the road with my daughter later that day to drive three hours to Eufaula, Alabama.

The girls called me to let me know they were on their way home. That was around 10:00 a.m. Check out wasn't until eleven. I wondered why they didn't stay and sleep as long as they could. But they thanked me for everything and told me they had a great time. I told them it was good meeting them again and matching their faces with their names, still a bit embarrassed for not knowing.

After I got a few more hours of sleep, Mani and I packed up and got on the road for my New Year's Eve event in Alabama.

It was a long, boring drive, but I talked to Allison almost the whole drive. I was glad she was on the phone with me because she kept me laughing the whole time.

Although it was a beautiful sunny day, it was freezing cold, even in Alabama. We finally arrived and it seemed like we were in the middle of nowhere. We had a little time to chill and relax because Alabama is an hour behind us, and because it was New Year's Eve, it wouldn't start until nine thirty or ten for watch night service.

The event started, and everyone was excited about the new year being just hours away. Everyone was really nice and seemed determined to take good care of us. They did a great job. This wasn't what you would call a big church, but for this small city, it was, and they apparently dreamed big too.

The event was filled with praise and worship and liturgical dance and me as the guest comedienne. They seemed to be excited to see "Chocolate" from *Def Comedy Jams* and *ComicView*. So I had a lot of fun with them. They were a great audience, and they seemed so appreciative of me being there. It made me feel good to bring in the new year with them.

Once we had all performed and the Word had gone forth and the new year was here, I shook some hands, gave some hugs, took some pictures, and kissed some babies (just kidding about the babies).

It was now 2006! To God be all glory! I never take going into a new year for granted.

I never take a day for granted. I'm grateful for every day God allows me to see. I'm always emotional to know that God's grace has brought us safely to this point in time. He didn't have to do it, and it's not because I deserve it, and many didn't live to see it. But here I stand alive and well in 2006, and my heart was grateful to see another year.

My new year's resolution is the same every year, to go higher in God, to be a more spiritually mature woman of God. To love more, laugh more, live more.

Little did I know that 2006 would go down as the darkest hour of my life.

The next morning, Mani and I got up and got on the road and headed back to Atlanta. On the way home, I called my best friend of thirty years (also my daughter's godmother) to wish her a happy New Year since I hadn't heard from her yet. Her name is Chinita too but spelled slightly different than mine. She invited us over for NYE dinner and fellowship because she had some other friends coming over as well and her family was in town. I accepted the invitation, but I had to wonder if we would've gotten one if I hadn't called her that day. Chinita and I are best friends because we have been friends or known each other since we were in the eighth grade. The only real reason we even hit it off was because we were the only two Chinnitas we knew. We hung in different crowds because we were from two very different sides of the tracks.

I grew up poor and in the hood of Gastonia, North Carolina. She grew up middle class. We both grew up with only sisters. She had three; I had five. She had both parents in the home; my mother was a single parent (although my dad was in my life). We had different fathers.

Chinita was really smart and hung out with the smarter kids at school. I was a "C" student, but I had a lot of common sense. So people thought I was smarter than I was. I went to school every day not because I loved it but because home was horrible and school was my safe haven.

I still have letters that Chinita and I wrote each other in junior high and high school. Silly letters, nothing serious. We really only talked in passing in the hallways at school. Never on the phone at home or anything like that.

When we graduated, Chinita went to East Carolina University, a PWC in North Carolina. I went to Livingstone College and transferred to Winston-Salem State University, both are HBCU's in North Carolina, and I joined the Marine Corps Reserves. We didn't see each other again until I moved to Atlanta and she moved there two years after I did. As soon as she got there, she called me. My auntie saw her at church and knew she was moving to Georgia and gave her my number. As soon as she called, I knew who she was. Even though we are from the same place and grew up together, Chinita had this really slow Southern accent that you don't normally hear from a black girl. I was elated to hear from her, and we hit it off immediately. We were inseparable. I had already started my comedy career, and she had moved down to work for one of the hospitals. We both flourished in our careers. We did life together and really walked out the best friend thing to a tee.

We were young and free. We partied, traveled, lived hard, laughed hard, and loved hard.

I got pregnant, married, divorced, and single again but now as a mom. Then I got saved. And I lived saved. And everything changed. I think this was the biggest turning point in our friendship. It was never the same after that and then the time apart grew further and further. And even though I would protest us not making time to see each other just a little more, my protests were in vain in spite of her promises to do better. Till this day, I love her something crazy, but I believe the best part of our friendship is over and has been for quite some time. It's just hard to admit it. We are still friends and will always be friends but "best" left our friendship at least ten years ago.

And New Year's Day 2006 opened my eyes more than anything before then. Regardless, we always loved and respected each other and pushed past any situation we were going through. No matter what, I knew I could always depend on Chinita to be there if I needed her in a clutch situation.

She was the first person I called when I found out I was pregnant. She was right there in the delivery room with me and my mother. She practically helped me raise my daughter the first two years of her life. She was there when I went through unimaginable foolishness with my first husband. She was the only one who knew how to deal with me when I went through bouts of depression stemming from flashbacks from my childhood. She knows everything about me—the good, the bad, and the ugly—and she still loves me unconditionally. And because of that, I will always love her something crazy. I'm not happy that the "best" part of friendship has run its course. I just believe that that season for us is up. And it is painful to admit. But I will take comfort in the fact that our friendship and love for each other is still strong and unwavering. It's just not the best we have to offer.

We may no longer operate in "best friend" realm, but she is definitely "my friend" and I think that's what matters most.

So now we were full-fledged into 2006 on day 2. Looking back over the past year, I must say I was blessed with some monumental moments that I will cherish in my heart. I got some things accomplished in 2005. But the two things that were highlights of that year for me were being licensed to preach by Pastor Aye in August. I preached my first sermon there and twenty-four people gave their lives to Christ that day. I can't say I expected that but to God be all glory! It feels amazing to be used by God. Of course, I was blessed to minister through comedy at Neicy Wray's all-girls conference. And since my divorce in 2003, this year will make three years for me being abstinent from sex. Now that may not mean a whole lot to you, but it's monumental for me. I didn't think I would make it a year, let alone three! But when I was going through my second divorce, God spoke to me and said "no dating," not until He allows it again. I wasn't happy about it but I wanted to be obedient and completely trust God in my relationships from now on. And thus far, it has proven to be what I needed. Because even though I'm not dating, I see things clearer now. I see the red flags, I see the games men play, and I'm able to recognize ungodly spirits and make better choices in men now. I see how sex can really cloud your judgment and have you falling for someone you know good and well God doesn't approve of for you.

I realize the importance of keeping your flesh under subjection; otherwise, you will make some really dumb decisions based on your flesh. And I can personally attest to that.

So here I am almost three years later, still single and celibate (that's a miracle from God within itself)! Thank you, Jesus!

Now I'm feeling pretty good about the new year, new life. I've been licensed for ministry and I'm just ready to go higher in Jesus. God is doing great things in my life. I'm getting my confidence and self-esteem back. I've had time to reassess some things and allow God to heal my broken heart and my broken spirit. My last divorce really took me down in my self-esteem. I've never been in an abusive relationship before, and it affects you vastly different than just regular marital problems. And it wasn't just physical abuse. It was verbal, mental, and emotional abuse. And my daughter had to witness all the pain I was experiencing although I tried to keep it from her. My first marriage was absolutely horrible. You just could've never told me in a million years that a man would stoop so low to get what they wanted out of pure selfishness. I mean, everything was predicated on a complete *lie*. I know I can be naive at times, but I just never thought people could be so dark in their hearts to manipulate people just to get what they want. People put on a great facade to come up, and they don't care whose head they have to step on to get there.

I didn't understand it at first, but after a while, I understood why God prohibited me from dating. I was learning and discerning more, and I became more patient in everything. I learned to really just wait on God.

Unfortunately, it took two train wrecks before I understood this wisdom. But that's kind of what happens when you have to go to the school of hard knocks because there was no one there to impart that kind of wisdom to me. No one. And so I basically learned relationships like I learned everything, through trial and error. But when I became a woman of God, I learned through the Word of God. So my error in my second marriage was believing that he was the man of God that he said he was and who he was portraying himself to be in church. That he would honor his vows to me and love me as Christ had commanded him to because he cared about obeying God's Word. But out of his own mouth, I would hear him tell me that "he lied at the altar," and that if he was out of God's will, then so be it. Wow!

Chapter 4
New Friends but Who Sent You?

Things were finally getting back to normal now that the new year had rolled in. Mani was back in school, and I was back to yucking it up on the phone with Allison. I was getting things done here and there—cooking, cleaning, preparing for upcoming events, and getting back into a workout regimen. Working out was important to me but I wasn't doing it to lose weight, I wanted to take care of my body but eat what I wanted to eat. Unfortunately, after my second divorce, I lost a lot of weight and became obsessed with gaining weight, on purpose. And I did. But I couldn't really see it and would continue to try to gain weight. My mother and my brother-in-law Robert were the only two who would say something to me about my weight. Still, I didn't see what they saw. So I kept eating and working out. LOL!

It was January so I didn't have a lot on the books. Work normally slows down after the holidays, especially in Christian comedy because not many churches are having events at the beginning of the year. But I did have a big Christian comedy conference coming up in Nashville, Tennessee. This was great news because Allison lives in Nashville and I will get to see her while I'm there.

This would be the first comedy conference of this magnitude for (African American) Christian comedians and they were doing it real big and pulling out all the stops. And it would be the same week as the Stellar Awards weekend. So I was really excited about that!

Now Allison and I would talk on the phone and make plans for my visit to Nashville, and once I got the itinerary for the whole week of the conference, we decided that we may try to go to the Stellar's but that she wanted me to stay over one night with her and her family and go to church with them that Sunday since the conference would be over on that Friday. We were acting like two teenage girls who looked forward to a sleepover.

Sheila was still calling, but not as much as she did before we all hung out in Gainesville. Not often but still frequent enough. Ironically, her friend Chloe had also started calling me on a regular basis. Not as much as Sheila did, but she would check in every now and again. I was kind of tickled that these young girls wanted to call and chitchat with me. And it was a bit entertaining as well in a strange way. However, Chloe's conversation was a little different from Sheila's. Chloe laughed a lot and was more upbeat. She seemed more confident and cool. And even though she was only twenty-two, she seemed wiser than her years.

She talked a lot about her friend Elizabeth or Liz as she called her. Like Allison and me, they met at the conference and had become the best of friends. Chloe always spoke so highly of her and how she never wanted to lose her friendship even though they had only been friends for a short time. She would always say after speaking of her "I luh dat chick!"

Talking to Chloe was kind of fun because of her personality. But I still had more fun talking to Allison. Chloe seemingly needed to talk and just release some things, which was why I felt like she had begun to call more regularly now too. It was cool, just like it was with Sheila. I didn't mind being the listening ear they needed, if that's what they needed. Besides, she was entertaining and had wit.

After about a week or more of Chloe calling and talking to me, one day I received a call from her and she was a bit more serious from the onset. More than usual and a bit somber if you will but as if she were trying to play it down. I asked her if she was okay. Trying to put a little more cheer in her voice, because she noticed that I noticed, she said, "Yes, yes, I'm fine, but I do need to talk to you." She said there was something she needed to tell me. At first, I was walking around multitasking, but this sounded serious like she needed my undivided attention so I went up to my bedroom and sat on the end of the bed with my feet up on the footboard. She seemed hesitant to speak, so I waited until she was ready, letting her know she could take her time. I asked her if she was okay. She said yes. I asked her if she was pregnant. She chuckled and assured me she was not.

Finally, she mustered up the courage to tell me that she was formerly a lesbian and how it had been two years since she gave up that lifestyle. I continued to listen. She went on to say that that was her past and that she had no desire to continue in it. That being at the conference really helped her overcome some anxieties about what she'd been through and that she was now living to draw closer to God.

Now I was relieved to hear this because, in her hesitance to speak, I have to admit I was thinking, "lawd this girl bout to tell me she gay!" I'm not gonna lie. I was thinking it because what else could be so hard to say except that maybe she was pregnant.

So then I began to ask her some questions to see if she was doing what was necessary to stay out of that lifestyle. She began telling me about a horrible car accident that she was in and how it made her rethink her choices in life. How she had now been living in Jacksonville with her godmother for the past two years and that her godmother was a minister of the Gospel and heavy into church. She told me how she grew up going to church with her mom and dad and her siblings.

We talked for a really long time that day. So much so that when Allison called, I told her I would call her back. I couldn't just leave her hanging off a cliff after she had confided something so private to me just to get on the phone and act silly with Allison. This was serious and it was ministry. I had to make sure she knew she could trust me. I wanted her to know that her past was just that, her past. And as long as she didn't come on to me, we would be fine. *No!* I was so serious, and I really did say it just like that. Not to be mean or anything close to it, but I needed her to know that up front. I wanted to handle that business before we went any further so we had that understanding down to a science. Again, she chuckled a little bit and assured me she wasn't attracted to me.

I reiterated to her that I'm not that way and that I don't agree with the lifestyle but that I loved her with the love of Christ and that if, at any time she needed to talk, I would be there for her.

Now I know some people are reading this and criticizing me for my response. Listen! This was twelve years ago and I'm just telling you how I responded at that time and I had a reason for making sure she wasn't attracted to me.

When I was in college, I was in marching band, and I had become really good friends with a young lady who unbeknown to me was a lesbian and I was just too incredibly naive to see it even when she wrote me a letter coming on to me. I thought it was just a really friendly letter and her being happy about our new friendship. Until one day, one of my big sisters on campus was in my room and the letter was on my desk and some of the wording caught her eye and she asked me if she could read it. I let her, and when she was finished, she asked me who this person was. I told her and she said, "You realize she is coming on to you?" I didn't really understand what she meant, and she just blurted out, "She likes you like a dude likes girls. She likes you!" She said it to me, laughing at me, and I responded, "No way!" So I went to this girl and asked her if that's what she was trying to convey to me, and she didn't deny it. She said it was. I told her that I wasn't that way, and if she was, I didn't have a problem with that and that we could still be friends but that I like men. She said she knew that and she understood and that she didn't mean to offend me. Less than a week later, I got another letter from her, but this time she was more straightforward and nothing to figure out. She plainly told me that if she couldn't have me, she didn't want to be around me. I was livid! I found her on campus, pulled her to the side and went off on her, and told her to stay as far away from me as she could and that if she saw me coming down the sidewalk, she'd better cross to the other side. Eventually, I forgave her, but we were never friends again.

Now I said all that to say that I didn't want to make the mistake of allowing Chloe to entertain the thought that she could come on to me.

So I wanted to nip it in the bud where the chick brought it up so there won't be any confusion. Now I really didn't have any problems with her past especially since now she has given her life to Christ. And I let her know that I will be here for her and she thanked me for that.

I still had some questions to ask, and she asked what did I want to know. Well, I know how highly she thought of Liz (her new best friend from the conference). They had become just as close as Allison and I, so I wanted to know if she had become attracted to Liz in some way. She told me she was in no way attracted to Liz and that she has never been attracted to girls her age but that she had always been attracted to women who were much older. She confided that her first lover was eighteen years older than she was and that her last lover was over forty years old. (Side-eye.) HOUSTON, WE HAVE A PROBLEM! Okay, wow! This was not okay! This was a *neon red flag*.

At this point, I felt a strong need to drive my point home, but trying not to be offensive, so once again, I let her know, "Now look... I know I'm fine and everything, but I really don't swing that way!" I tried to chuckle just a bit so as to not offend her, but I was so serious, and I meant what I said. She laughed a little bit too and reassured me that she was done with that lifestyle and that she was not attracted to me.

So now we are less than a week away from the Christian comedy conference in Nashville, Tennessee, and they had big things planned for all who would attend. I was to teach a segment at the conference and also do stand-up for a live taping. They flew a few of us up and put us up at the host hotel (which was really nice and posh). It was like a reunion for those of us who had not seen each other in a long time and a meet and greet for the new comics on the scene.

It was really cold in Nashville. I think it even snowed while we were there.

Being that I now talked to Sheila and Chloe regularly, they both knew that I was going to the conference in Nashville and was happy that I would get to spend some time with my good friend Allison.

Chloe now seemed to call me more than Sheila did and was even beginning to cut in to Allison's time. I don't know if Allison noticed it but I did, and I thought it was a bit peculiar, but I didn't make much of it. Because sometimes when she and I would talk, we would address the "elephant in the room," her sexual preference. And it was almost like she was using me to listen to her get it off her chest, so to speak.

She told me how it began for her as a young teenager. I noticed how she had gotten to a place where she was comfortable discussing it with me. I wasn't uncomfortable with it, but I wasn't really comfortable with it either. It was almost as if she enjoyed giving me information about it. Sometimes, to change the tone, I would kind of tease her about it because I just couldn't grasp the concept at all. She would laugh, and I wasn't sure if she was laughing at me teasing her or laughing at me because I was so naive.

By the time I got to the conference in Nashville, Chloe was calling as much as Allison was and now she was keeping me on the phone longer. I was spending more time on the phone now more than I ever had because of my newfound friends from the conference last year. Before then, I really was not one to spend hours on the phone. This was new for me, and being that I have a young daughter, sometimes it took up too much of my time. But it was hard to say no to my newfound friends, and because it's normally just Mani and me, I actually enjoyed the company and conversation. I had people to share the details of my day with who actually cared to hear about them. With Allison, it was like iron sharpening iron. We both seemed to be well versed in scripture, so when we talked about life and its challenges and unwanted changes, we always did so with the Word of God in mind. As silly as we could be with one another, we both enjoyed talking about the Word of God. However, with Sheila and Chloe, it was more like ministry. Here were two young girls just trying to figure this life thing out and serve God along the way who needed someone to hear them out in the process and hopefully answer some questions they might have without judging them.

Now I must admit that, in the beginning, I thought I was just a really cool person to talk to and I must be really good at helping people, but I do forget that people get excited about my platform. I never look at myself as a celebrity or public figure. So sometimes, I completely forget about that part. And so I forget that sometimes people are attracted to what you do and not who you are.

And I admit that in this situation, I completely forgot that that could be a possibility. Even though there were times when each one of them would bring up watching me on *Def Comedy Jams* or *Comic View* years ago and we would laugh about something I had said. Chloe and Sheila both would tell me how they would sneak away with their siblings and watch us on HBO and BET knowing they weren't supposed to be watching because they were much too young at the time. We would just laugh about it and go on to the next conversation. It didn't dawn on me until later that some of the attraction from all three of them was because of my platform and that maybe, I wasn't as great as I thought I was. LOL!

Chapter 5
There's More To It

I got to the conference and was elated to see so many of my friends and colaborers in Christian comedy that I had not seen in a while. We all hugged and joked around with each other (it just happens naturally with comedians). They got us checked into our rooms and rounded everyone back together in the lobby shortly after. I could already tell this was going to be fun by how organized it was.

I called my daughter to let her know I'd made it and that I would call her when Allison came to get me. She was as excited as I was that I would get to hang out with Allison and her daughter. The only down part to this was that I would be away from my daughter for a week. But I knew she would be in good hands with Tia.

The conference was only three days, but we had to get there a day early, and I was staying an extra two days to hang out with Allison and her daughter for a day and maybe go to the Stellar Awards on that Saturday, which also happened to be my mother's sixtieth birthday.

I was torn between staying for the Stellars or going home for my mother's birthday. She wanted me to come home for her birthday party. My only reservation with that was all the traveling I would do to get there and my mom was still in the world and I didn't go to her parties. The last time she had talked (guilted us) us into going to her birthday bash when everything in me told me not to go, I wind up having a bad roll-over accident and totaled my SUV. Praise God no one was hurt. But we were pretty shaken up.

I had my daughter, my two nephews, and my oldest sister riding with me, and it began to snow. I kept telling my sister that I didn't think this was a good idea. It just didn't feel right, and it wasn't nothing holy about this party. My thing was, if you're as grateful to God as you claim to be for gracing you with another year, then why aren't you giving Him the glory instead of the hanging out with the enemy.

Long story short, I went against my intuition and we wind up having a horrible wreck. And the sad part is, they went on and had the party any way. So since that time, I decided if she wasn't doing something I felt comfortable doing, then I wasn't driving all the way to North Carolina to sit around listening to loud, obnoxious music while people were drinking and smoking. I would just have to send her something instead. Although I did wrestle with it all week as to whether or not I would go because it was her sixtieth.

Once everyone got checked into their rooms, we all met back up in the lobby to go over the itinerary for the next three days.

Allison was coming to pick me up from the hotel to meet her mother. I had actually met her at the conference because she helped with my T-shirt sales. But as I stated earlier, if I didn't spend significant time with you, I'm bad at remembering. But we have spoken over the phone since Allison and I have become friends.

So after we all met in the lobby and went over the itinerary, we just mingled among each other and did some networking. I thought, this was so cool to be among my colleagues in Christian comedy.

This is the coolest job or ministry I could've ever dreamed of, and here I was with people who labor with me and love sharing the joy of Jesus unashamedly and glorifying God with our gifts. We are blessed to do what we do and it's no easy task, because unlike secular comedy, you can't just say anything you want to say. You are not only held to a higher standard in comedy but also in your life as a Believer. We are comedians, but this walk is not a joke to us. We take it very seriously. Most of us anyway.

This is not for the faint at heart. Many comedians who do comedy don't like being labeled "Christian comedian" because they feel it limits their work and they try to discourage others from doing it as well, saying we are shooting ourselves in the foot calling ourselves Christian comedians. I knew what it would mean when I took on the title, but I did it because I was led to by God. Not to be super spiritual but because God said so. And I trust Him. And maybe that's not what God spoke to the others, but for me that's the charge He gave me. And obedience to God means everything to me.

See I didn't start out doing clean or Christian comedy. I started out in the secular where I got paid a lot of money to talk a lot of foolishness. And this made me famous for about six years of the eight that I was doing secular comedy. But in 1998, God called me in out of darkness at a time when life was great for me! I was making more money than I ever dreamed of, touring the world and being celebrated. I had made some major TV appearances that made my name (alter ego "Chocolate") famous and life was grand!

But when God spoke to my heart, I said yes. And I've never regretted my decision to do so, not for a moment since.

Allison had arrived at the hotel to pick me up. She mingled with me and some of the other comedians for a minute and I think one of them struck her fancy, but when I let him know, he told me he was already in a relationship. On the surface, I thought they would make a really cute couple, so I was a little bummed out that he turned down my friend. Oh well.

Allison and I left to go to her house to meet her mom and dad, who were really cool people and had obviously been married for a long time. I love to see beautiful marriages. It blesses my heart. I pray to have a beautiful marriage myself someday soon.

So Allison, and her mom, and I sat around and talked for a few hours, but it had gotten late and her daughter was staying over one of her relatives' house so Allison came and stayed with me at the hotel. We stayed up late talking and watching T.V. until we fell asleep.

The next morning, she got up and left early because she had somethings to do. I stayed in bed just a little longer because, for one, that bed was so plush and comfortable it was ridiculous! And the room had an ambiance that made you want to stay in bed. That's not good, is it? But I had to get up, get showered, and get ready because the seminars were starting at 11:00 a.m. and we would all meet for breakfast before then.

So after breakfast, we were in seminars most of the day for the first day. They were really interesting and enlightening seminars.

But it's hard for seminars to be boring when you've got comedians teaching them. And it's impossible when your audience is a bunch of comedians. LOL!

During one of the early afternoon seminars, my phone rang, and it took me a minute to get it to shut it off because I had no intentions of answering it during the seminar. I was scrambling to shut it off quick because it was embarrassingly loud, and when I finally got it off, I saw that it was just Chloe calling. However, about two minutes later, my phone rang again. Again, I scrambled to turn it off. Let me add that it was one of those "new" upscale flip phones. And I'm not techno savvy so I didn't know how to put the ringer on silence or vibrate. But again, it was Chloe. No one said anything and they pretty much tried to act like they didn't notice the interruptions, but I was still a bit embarrassed. And I did my best to look apologetic for the interruptions and show my interest in the seminar despite my disrupting the class with my phone. And as if it were not already bad enough, it rang again, and again it was Chloe. Okay, maybe it's an emergency if she's called back to back like that. I better step out and take it. I left the class and closed the door behind me to answer the call, praying whatever the emergency, it was nothing bad. But when I answered, she very casually asked me what I was doing. I told her I was in a seminar and asked her was everything okay because surely there is an emergency for you to have called me back to back like that. She said, "Oh no, why did you think something was wrong?"

"Because you just called me three times back to back!"

She laughed. "I'm sorry, I was just calling to see what you were doing. Did I disturb you?"

"Chloe, you know I'm at this conference. Yes, you disturbed me and everybody else!"

I sound a little perturbed now because I am. She's laughing harder now. "I'm sorry. I apologize, I didn't meant to disturb you guys," she said (still chuckling).

I chuckled a little too so as to not sound too upset. "I will call you when I'm done."

"Okay," she said, "please forgive me."

"No, problem, I'll call you later." I hung up and went back into the seminar. What did I miss? Questions are going back and forth like I missed something important. One question sparks another and comedians are engulfed in learning more and I'm loving the banter. Everybody is partaking at this point and we are gleaning from each other. And then it happens, my phone makes that loud T-Mobile text message noise. Again, it was Chloe. *Really!* I'm shaking my head with a half smile like what does this girl want? Did she forget to tell me something because I did kind of rush her off the phone?

Well, in the midst of the back-and-forth banter among the comedians, they wouldn't notice me checking my phone. When I looked to see what she had texted, I didn't really grasp it. It read, "I can't get you out of my head." LOL! I laughed a little bit and quickly text her back to "Leave me alone. I'll call you later." LOL!

She sent me a smiley-face emoji, which made another loud T-Mobile text noise when it came through.

And in the midst of the class with all the commotion going on around me, something in my spirit spoke to me and said, "There is more to that text than you comprehend."

Then I began to ponder what she said in the text: "I can't get you out of my head." Surely, I thought, she cannot be attracted to me. Naaaaaaw! Don't think like that. She knows better than that.

We've already discussed this, and she knows I'm not that way. Certainly not! No way... can't be! She's just being a sweetheart. Yeah, just being nice.

But "there's more to it" kept resonating in my spirit and wouldn't let me go. It made me uneasy for the rest of the day. Now I wondered if I needed to address this.

After the class was over, I called and talked to her for a quick second but told her I couldn't talk long because Allison was on her way to get me so we could go to lunch and hang out for a little bit and that I would call her when I got back to my room. She said that was fine. I commenced to talking and mingling with the other comics while I waited on Allison to pull up outside. I was thoroughly enjoying the conference but really ecstatic about spending some hang time with my girl Allison. We had more fun in person than we did on the phone. She was a lot of fun to be around. I thanked God for her. She was refreshing to my life. When you are a single woman or parent, it helps to have someone walk with you who understands your struggles, who you can share your heart with, and someone who will listen with understanding. We would talk about our exes and things we experienced in our marriages and our expectations for our future husbands and how we looked forward to being in loving marriages. We were praying for one another because we wanted each other to have the blessings that we desired.

    I had grown to love Allison like a little sister that I could really relate to and I felt like I could trust her with my heart. She seemed to be a lot like me. She thought it was cool that I took time with Chloe and Sheila to make sure they were okay whenever they needed to talk considering I had my own problems. But truthfully, that just came naturally for me. I try to be for people what I wish I had when I was coming up so that I wouldn't make some of the mistakes I had to make in order to learn from them. I wish someone would've taken the time to speak wisdom into my life. But there was no one. There were people who loved me I guess. But either they didn't have the wisdom, or they didn't have the time—or both. So it's hard for me to ignore people when they may be in need and I have the means to help. And as many times as I have been burned, you would think that I wouldn't be so giving but I don't want to say no and it's the one person who needed me the most. God is my avenger.

    It felt like Allison was becoming my new "best" friend, but Chinita was not yet willing to relinquish that title, and I wasn't so sure I was ready for her to. We had grown up together in our teens, our twenties, our thirties. We had too much invested, and as angry as I was that we never made time for each other anymore, I was crazy about Chinita. We talked so seldom now. She didn't even know about Allison. The only times I would see Chinita now was maybe my birthday (if she didn't forget again), maybe her birthday (if she had the time), but definitely Mani's birthday. But to be honest, it blessed my heart for her to fight for our friendship the day after New Year's, even though at this point she still wasn't showing any signs of stepping up. Through my tears, I agreed to hang on though my heart was breaking because I could see that we had drifted so far apart.

But I knew that if I ever needed her, she would be right there without hesitation. Unfortunately, I did need her. No, I had no emergency situation or any situation. I just needed some quality time with my friend for no reason at all.

I guess you can tell that I love hard. As many times as I have had my heart broken in love, marriage, relationships, friendships, family, you name it, it has never made me bitter or jaded. If you win my friendship or my heart, I tend to give my all. I have learned a lot so it definitely doesn't happen quickly and I am most definitely more cautious now than I've ever been but I'm all in or all out. I don't do anything halfway. Unfortunately, I expect the same in return, but most people don't understand true friendship or true commitment. And coming to that realization has taught me better to guard my heart with diligence.

So at this time in my life, nearly three years divorced, celibate, and trusting God for my man of God and yet holding on. It was good to meet a friend who was not only living for God as well but loving it and desiring spiritual maturity as much as I did. Someone who could relate to the same convictions I had. That's one thing Chinita and I did not have. I didn't let it hinder our friendship, but I can't say the same for her.

Allison and I had a great time hanging out that day, but it was getting late and she had to be up early, and so did I. She dropped me back off at the hotel, and when I got back to my room, I started going over the material I would be presenting for my portion of the seminar tomorrow afternoon.

While going over some of the notes, I remembered that I needed to call Chloe back. What she'd texted me earlier just didn't sit well in my spirit and kind of disturbed my peace.

I was still wondering if I should address it and ask her if she was becoming attracted to me. I didn't want to, but I felt like I might need to just to make sure we nipped it in the bud if she was beginning to think like that.

On the other hand, what if I ask her that and I was dead wrong and she gets offended. God knows I don't want to offend her. She probably has to deal with people always accusing her of being attracted to them when she was just being nice. She probably has to walk on eggshells with everyone she meets just so they don't think or assume she's making a pass at them. I didn't want to make her feel like she needed to walk on eggshells, but I don't want her to be attracted to me either.

I know from some of the conversations we've had on the phone that she's been through some things so she could be fragile. So if I was going to ask her this, I'd better be sure this was God telling me to. And I wasn't.

So when I did call her that evening, I did not mention it. But I did jokingly ask her what did she mean she couldn't get me out of her head and why not. Why was I stuck in her head? She laughed her little coy twenty-two-year-old laugh and told me how much she enjoyed talking to me and that she learned so much from me. And how she could tell that I was a minister because I always ministered to her. How some things she didn't really care to hear but she knew she needed to. We wind up talking for a couple of hours that night and we'd talked a long time the night before.

I wasn't happy about her keeping me up late, but in reality, I was the one being so irresponsible. Staying up late on the phone knowing it would make me sleep late and I had a conference to attend. That was not wisdom. But I get reeled in by good conversations and we always had good conversations. We talked about God and His will for our lives. We talked about my situation and me being divorced twice and being a single parent. And she was a good listener as well. She had a comforting spirit, and she actually seemed to care about the things that have hurt me and things that concerned me.

We talked about Allison and how our friendship blossomed since the conference last year. We talked about her friend Liz and how they've practically become best friends in a matter of months and how much she adored their friendship. She talked about how cool Liz was and how much she had going on in her life and how involved she was with the kids in her community and how much of a

Neicy Wray fan Liz was. She once told me she asked God if she could keep her, and she laughed afterward. Because she said, people tend to come and go in her life just when she seems to get attached to them. So this was a friendship she hoped she'd never lose.

I thought that was really sweet of her and even more so of Liz that her character would be so strong and positive as to bring a sincere comradery to a wandering soul. Like I said before, she was wise beyond her years. But I did need to show more discipline and stop staying up late on the phone.

Chapter 6
Something in My Spirit Ain't Right

When we hung up the phone that night, I fell off to sleep immediately. But I was a little angry for not having the discipline to get off the phone earlier knowing I will pay for it in the morning.

I got up late rushing to get dressed, again angry about my lack of discipline. I did get to the seminar on time, but we started a little late. Apparently, some of the other comedians needed more time too. I sat through a couple of classes before it was time for a lunch break, but when we get back, it would be my turn to speak. The topic chosen for me by the committee was "Living Holy in the Entertainment Industry." I was excited about the topic, but I was glad we were breaking because I needed to go to my room and regroup. Something in my spirit wasn't right.

I was being bombarded with thoughts of me needing to ask Chloe if everything was okay with our friendship and to make sure she wasn't becoming attracted to me.

Not only that but my body was feeling super weird and was just kind of doing its own thing.

My flesh was cutting up something terrible and I had no clue why. This was really strange.

So I went back to my room so that I can take some time to pray and go over my notes. I took any opportunity to speak very seriously, especially when it comes to God and His people. And I always wanted to operate in the power of God's anointing. I wanted to deliver a message that would bless and encourage them to stand for righteousness no matter how good or bad things got in the industry. But as much as I prayed and go over my notes, something in my spirit was just not right. I mean, I was really bothered, so much so that I literally began to cry and wasn't sure why. I felt like there was a strong interference in my spirit and I prayed, "God, help me. What is this?" It seemed like my flesh had turned up a thousand watts. This had never happened to me before in my life, not for no reason, and all of a sudden. I was baffled. Now I was scared. I've got to go do this seminar, and my flesh was on fire! None of this was making sense.

Was it something I ate? Could something I ate do that? And on top of all that was this sense of urgency to ask Chloe if she was becoming attracted to me. I believe there may have been some things said on the phone last night that brought me back to wondering again. Or it could be the fact that she's kept me up on the phone all night for the past two nights that's raised an eyebrow. Whatever the reason, I know hands down that when I talk to her later today, it must be addressed. I gathered myself together after fervently praying for the Holy

Spirit to have His way in me at this conference to speak wisdom into the lives of these young comedians who desire to use their gifts for God's glory. I prayed that we would all be better at worshiping Him in a more excellent way. I pulled myself together, wiped my tears (tears that came from worrying if I would bring God glory with my words and fear of this unknown sudden interference with my body). How can I worship like this?

Praise God everything was located in the hotel so we could walk from our rooms to the conference halls.

I was supposed to speak for an hour, including taking questions. But because we were behind schedule with the seminars, I had to share my hour with another comedian, which now gave me only thirty minutes. This actually worked to my advantage. But I had written so much material that now I would have to break down the most important areas to speak on for thirty minutes.

Once I got to the podium, I was okay but still felt weird especially in my body so I was still praying for the power of the Holy Spirit to manifest. I always enjoy teaching on the things of God. Jesus is my favorite subject. I love learning more and more about God. I figure since Jesus is the Word made flesh, the more I consume the Word of God, the more I become like Christ.

I took great pleasure in teaching my segment, but I felt like I may be being way too serious about everything. But it's hard for me to not show my passion when I'm talking about my Father. Besides, it must've been quite interesting because I got a lot of questions. Then I began to get emotional from responding to one of the questions. I can't remember what the question was, but I know I had to respond by telling my redemption story and how it hasn't been easy and how I was grateful for God's keeping power because of how work for me had slowed down because of my stand for Christ. I spoke about how hurt I was to be hanging in the balance because the secular had stopped booking me and churches hadn't really started, how I was glad that I had money put up because for the most part (through the Grace of God), that's what sustained me.

As I got emotional, I saw that some of the other comedians were becoming emotional as well. Many of them knew my testimony of being at a very high place in my career in secular comedy and at that time showed no signs of slowing down anytime soon. And I was making hundreds of thousands of dollars and life was great. It wasn't tragedy that brought me to Christ. It was just me hearing His voice and the conviction in my heart that made me know that all the money and fame in the world meant nothing if my soul was perishing. I needed Jesus! So I walked away from it all to serve God, and I have not regretted it one moment of my life since I made the choice.

I believe many of them could understand my heart and my hurt from not feeling like I was finally accepted by the church after so many years of faithfully walking with God. I committed my life to Christ in the latter part of 1998. Here it was eight years later, and work was extremely patchy with the church and I was yet holding on. But I also believe they could relate because most of us Christian comedians were vying for the churches to recognize us and respect our gifts.

When the events and seminars for that day were over, I retreated back to my room to relax and eat. My part was finally done, praise

God! I get real tense when I have to minister, so I was happy to be done and relaxing in my room. I needed this time alone.

However, I knew that even though I needed to relax, this issue with Chloe still needed to be addressed. And although I was worried that I could be very wrong and could risk offending her, I knew it was a chance I had to take just to clear the air and make sure this wasn't going to be a problem.

Or else my spirit would be burdened until I dealt with it.

So as I settled in my room after having room service, I knew she would soon call, so I waited for her to call me. It didn't take long before my phone was ringing. My heart was beating fast as I wondered how long I would allow us to talk before I asked her the question. Not to mention, my body was still feeling weird.

I knew I didn't want to be on the phone all night again, so I'd better find a way to bring it up. As I mustered up the courage to ask this (what I thought was insulting, but just to make sure) question, that I was praying I was wrong about, my heart began to beat faster, but here goes nothing! "Lord, please don't let her be offended."

I prefaced my question with "I have to ask you something but please do not get mad, and if you have any questions, please let me explain before you start going off." She agreed. I began, "I respect who you are and all that you have overcome, but something has been burdening my spirit for the past two days." Even though I had introduced the question, it was really hard for me to present it. Ugh! I really didn't want to offend her. I continued to hesitate. How would I respond if she said no and got upset? I didn't want to upset her. I didn't want to set her back and make her feel like I was judging her by her past, and no matter how hard she tried, she would always be perceived that way. I wanted to be the last person that made her feel like she would always live under a microscope because of her past. Yet and still, I needed to know what was going on in her head. Because if the answer was yes, again, "Houston, we have a problem!"

I have prefaced the question but I was still hesitating because I had to consider what I would do if she did say yes. Would I respond in anger? Would I be more mature spiritually and talk to her calmly to reiterate that I'm not that way? Or would I simply end our friendship right then and there?

After all, I had been here before with the girl in college. And I had no clue she was "that way." But after the situation went down with her and we were no longer friends, when I would see her around campus, I did realize that she was very boyish. How I overlooked that before, I'm not sure. Maybe because I just didn't really know if it meant anything. I'm not sure. I personally don't think I noticed it until I knew for a fact that she was gay. On the other hand, Chloe is a very feminine young lady, and had she never told me she was "that way" before, I would've never thought that about her. To me, she's even more feminine than me.

Well, I've set the stage to ask the question, and I've hesitated long enough—*ask the question already, before my heart jumps out of my chest!*

She was waiting patiently almost as if she knew what I was about to ask. So I took a deep breath, and as articulate as I could be (so I wouldn't have to repeat myself), I asked her, "Are you becoming attracted to me?"

For a good moment, complete silence. I began to wonder, *Did she hear me?* She must have because she hasn't asked me to repeat myself, so that can't be it. Still no response yet. I continued to wait without saying anything because I didn't want to risk us both beginning to talk at the same time if she decided to answer.

Still silence... and now I'm pretty sure I've offended her and she's probably trying to keep from cussing me out, which wouldn't be so bad because, at least, that would mean that I was wrong and she's not attracted to me, right?

Still nothing. Maybe now might be a good time to repeat the question just in case. But something in me said, "Wait for it—she heard you." So I continued to wait... and finally, she began to speak. She didn't answer yes or no. She just began to go back over the night she and Sheila came to Gainesville, Florida, to see my show on December 30, 2005. I was a bit baffled but decided to just listen to see where this was going. She talked about how much fun she had in my presence. How cool it was to scroll through my Bible and see how well read it was. She said she was intrigued by my kindness and how pretty she thought I was, especially after I came out of the bathroom after my shower and the pretty pajamas I had on made me even more radiant. (These are her words.) She talked about how she loved how we laughed so much that night. She began to explain how, on their way home, when she and Sheila had parted ways, how overwhelming her feelings had become. So much so that she began to cry and she called a friend while she was driving and crying to let her know what just happened and what was going on with her feelings. She confided her feelings for me to this person who was one of very few people that knew of her past lifestyle. She said her friend tried to calm her down while she was trying to explain her attraction to me and how sweet she thought I was. (Lump in my throat, my intuition was right— ugh! Help me, Holy God!)

She said her friend told her not to allow her flesh to go there, that she was reading too much into it, and that she was sure I was just being nice. (Side-eye because I'm trying to figure what I did to make her think otherwise.)

I kept silent and listened very carefully to all she had to say as she continued to speak and was near tears in her explanation. While she spoke, I also pondered "What say I to all of this, because, in a nutshell, her answer was simply yes. Yes, she is attracted to me.

DOGGONIT! NOW WHAT? I'm not a cusser, but I really wanted to cuss. But I was diligent to keep calm so as not to hurt her feelings. But how do I respond to this? I'm angry, but I can't let her know that. I know to keep quiet because I don't want to say something I'm going to regret or hurt her feelings.

This cannot be happening. How? Why? You promised me you wouldn't! I didn't say it, but I was definitely thinking it and clenching my teeth. I was angry and vexed in my spirit, but I kept silent until I could speak reasonably. So here again we sit in this awkward silence because it's my turn to speak and I'm speechless. (Not really, but what I have to say is not godly.)

I know that I have to calm my spirit and find a way to respond with kindness. I prayed under my breath, "Father, help me to respond according to your will." I needed to say something soon or she would begin to think I was angry (and she would be right, but I didn't want her to know that).

She began to cry. This really bothered me because I didn't want to be the reason she was hurting. Man, this is not what I bargained for! Why is this happening? Well, I got to say something because it was heartbreaking to hear her crying. I think she may be crying because she's disappointed in herself for the setback. I'm not sure why she's crying, and at this point, I want to cry because I'm angry and I have to play nice. It's hard but I know I have to handle this fragile situation with care. I have to choose my words carefully even though this frustrates me to no end.

I'm really trying to speak, but I have no words to say. I guess she realized that I couldn't talk and took it upon herself to speak first. She asked me was I mad at her. I responded, "No, I'm not [not sure that was true], but I don't understand how this happened if you've been free from this for two years now." I then asked her if there was something that I did that made her think I was that way. Because if it was, I didn't want to do it again ever. She said no. Her reasons she said was because I was so nice and thoughtful toward them that night and that I've been a blessing to her since she's been communicating with me. I then asked, "So do you fall for anyone that is nice to you often?"

"Not at all," she said. "I was trying so hard not to, but my feelings got the best of me." She then went on to apologize quite a few times. I'm sure she could sense my great disappointment. She asked me if she should go away and forget about our friendship. Wisdom would've said yes, but I was too worried about hurting her feelings, so I said, "No, that won't be necessary. We will get through this. The enemy is testing you." She agreed.

I told her we would not allow the devil to get the victory in this and that with God on our side, we would get through this. Again, she agreed. However, I felt the need to reiterate to her that "I'm not that way. I'm not gay." She said she knew that and again apologized for feeling like she did.

We got off the phone, and though it was still a bit early evening, the night went long for me because when we hung up, I sat there in disbelief trying to figure out how this happened. Going over and over in my head the night they came to Gainesville to see me and what I may have done that night to lead her to feel the way she does. Or what have I said over the phone conversations that may have led her to feel that way. I'm wracking my brain trying to figure out what I did wrong. But I kept coming up with nothing. All I can think of is that she looks up to me because I minister to her from time to time. Maybe she just admires my stand for Christ. I've shared my testimony with her and maybe it gives her strength to keep pressing and maybe she is confusing her admiration for me with lust. Maybe this is just a schoolgirl-type crush on her teacher, and it just happens to be same sex because that's normal for her. I believe that's probably more than likely what it is, a schoolgirl crush on her mentor. Yeah, that's got to be it. I was convinced that was it and I had figured out the problem, and surely, we could get pass this now that we know what it is. And I couldn't wait to share it with her, that it's just a crush girl. You will get over it.

But I had no intentions of calling her back tonight because I was already tired and sleepy, and it wouldn't be wise to stay up late tonight knowing we had a big day tomorrow that I need to be prepared for. Because the conference would end tomorrow night, a Thursday, with a big comedy show taping for television on Friday and I needed to get my head in the game. Tapings always make me crazy nervous! However, I did talk to Allison before going to bed that night, but it was really brief because we were both very tired.

Chapter 7

James 1:20
Human Anger Doesn't Produce God's Righteousness

The next day, we finished up the seminars and did a mini-comedy audition to see what new comic would open for the comedy live taping tomorrow night. Then we had a few hours to go get lunch. Some people went out for lunch, and some ate at the hotel. I went back to my room because I wanted to make a quick call to Chloe to make sure she was doing okay and to tell her what I'd come to conclude about her attraction to me.

When I called, she seemed happy to hear from me and was a little more relaxed now. Her voice just above a whisper. She talked very carefully, almost as if she were afraid for some reason. I asked if she was okay, and she said she was better, and she asked me how I was feeling and what I was thinking. I told her I was fine and that I had been thinking a lot about the situation, and I began to tell her how I felt about it.

How I felt like she was just a young girl with a schoolgirl crush on someone she has grown to admire and look up to. I told her that normally, that's cute and okay, but not when it's same sex and the other person isn't gay. But I believed that, like any schoolgirl crush, it would subside and that I thought that she would eventually be okay but that she had to be mindful not to think that way about me because I'm not that way.

I felt like the Holy Spirit had really given me the words to say and to deliver it in a way that was so eloquent that her feelings would be spared and she could completely understand and agree with me. Surely, my theory was a home run. That ball was out of the park and I heard the cheers of a thousand angels screaming, "Team Jesus! Hallelujah!" And the clouds parted in the blue sky and that brilliant ray of sunlight shone down from heaven. LOL! But that's how great I thought I had conveyed my theory. And I sat up shoulders squared with the attitude of "What say ye to these things?" Like yeah, I figured it out and I'mma shut this down now because God knows I'm not interested in that at all. So the devil is a liar, and I cast this foolishness back down to the pit of hell from whence it came. Now of course, I didn't say all that, but I was thinking it.

And just when my spirit began to celebrate what I considered a home run, she leaped higher than I ever imagined she would and snatched my theory right out of midair by responding with "I understand how you could think that and I've tried to look at it from different angles too. So I know better. I know it's not just a schoolgirl crush, Chinnita. I know how I feel and I have fallen in love with you."

(Insert screeching tires here.)

EXCUSE ME! COME AGAIN! WHAT DO YOU MEAN YOU HAVE FALLEN IN LOVE WITH ME? Long pause from me... clenching teeth and tight fist. This girl was determined to upset me!

Now I'm livid and about to lose it! At this point, for some reason, I lost all concern for her feelings. I went in! And it wasn't pretty. She began to try to make her point and I wasn't trying to hear it. Now I was angry and I couldn't hide it. This was preposterous to me. There is no way you could be in love with me. "Why would you say that? Now you are tripping and you must be playing games! No, you betta be playing games li'l girl, 'cause this ain't even funny!" (Yes, this was said aloud.)

She wanted desperately for me to calm down and reminded me that it was almost time for me to go back to the conference and that we could finish the conversation later. I agreed very angrily, and we hung up. My blood was boiling! I prayed and tried to get my spirit right before going back out to the conference.

I didn't need this foolishness in my life. I had enough that I was already dealing with while I was at the conference. Preparing for the seminars, being away from my daughter for a week, my mother's birthday, and I had yet to figure out what I was getting her or if I would make the drive to be at her party. Not to mention the big taping tomorrow night, and for some reason, my flesh was cutting up something crazy! I didn't know why or what was going on with my body, but it was reeling and I'd never experienced anything like it before, not just for no reason. I thought maybe because I was turning forty soon. Couldn't be my cycle. I'd just had that a week before. I don't know, but it was really annoying. So I really didn't need some little girl coming on to me right now. *Who does that? Are you serious?* Not cool, little girl! Not cool at all!

I was next to useless on the last leg of the seminars. All I could think about was getting back on the phone to straighten her out. And the more I thought about it, the more I realized, *She lied to me from the very beginning*. She knew she was attracted to me when she called me after seeing me in Gainesville, Florida. So this did not just start over the past two weeks or so. This made me even more upset.

Once the last of the seminars were over for that day, I went back to my room and did all that I needed to do before settling down to talk to her to get to the bottom of this.

I had to call my daughter to make sure all was well with her and that she was being a good girl and doing well in school. She and Tia (my sitter) were fine and in good spirits. I had to call my mom to check on her. My mother and I talk every day. She is my best friend now, but there was a time when we had no relationship at all. She was very abusive to me when I was a child. But God turned that relationship completely around. (That's another book.) But like best friends, we have our differences, as we did this day, which was the last thing I needed right now. As we chatted for a bit, she asked me if I would make it home for her birthday party on Saturday. My answer wasn't quite what she wanted to hear, but it wasn't an absolute no either. I love my mom, but right now she's not really talking about a whole lot and I still have another call to make before I can get on the phone with Chloe and get some insight on why she lied to me from the beginning.

Mom and I finally said our "I love yous" and hung up. So now I got to call my girl Allison to make sure we are still on for tomorrow with her and her daughter coming to the taping and me staying over with them on Saturday. I hadn't mentioned the situation with Chloe to her yet although I knew I would. Now was not a good time because she had to go to work early in the morning so we didn't stay on the phone long.

Now it was time to get to the bottom of this foolishness. So I got my pajamas on and prepared myself for bed, because after this conversation, I was going to straight to sleep. This whole situation has me exasperated already.

I called, and she was apparently waiting for my call. It didn't take long for her to pick up. The conversation started off civil enough although I think she knew I was perturbed about this mess. As much as I tried to stay civil, it wasn't long before I was upset again. I told her that she lied to me from the beginning because she knew that she was attracted to me the first time she called me after they had seen me in Gainesville. I had told her when she confided in me her past sins that I wasn't that way and to please not come on to me. I told her that I felt like she had planned this all along and that I hate it when people lie to me. And I really do. I hate when people feel like they have to lie to you to have you in their life. And I believe she knew what she was doing the whole time. Maybe she didn't feel that way until she saw me in Gainesville, but nonetheless, she knew how she felt when she began to call me after the new year. And here I was thinking she was a really cool kid who, like Sheila, just needed someone to talk to. And I'm just being me availing myself to what I thought was this young lady needing someone to listen to her hurt and her pain and love her regardless of her past.

At this point I'm really angry. Even more so than I was earlier. More than I was even when the girl in college came on to me the second time.

And now she's talking and trying to get with me by being smart-mouthed and arguing back, but I would cut her off and cut her down.

I had no sympathy. I was furious and could only see red, and unfortunately, it wasn't because of the blood of Jesus.

It seemed the more she talked, the angrier I got because she was pretty slick at the mouth too to be so young. And if I didn't know any better, I would think she was insinuating that I should've known or did know. *Really, chick!* Man, I could've jumped through that phone and choked this little girl. How dare she try to blame me for this. How are you going to blame someone for not knowing what they don't know! God as my witness, I was completely oblivious until she sent the text, saying, "I can't get you out of my head." And even then, it didn't register immediately. But praise God, discernment kicked in and said, "There is more to that text than what you are reading."

The last thing I ever wanted this young lady to think was that I had anything gay about me. Because I didn't and wasn't trying to. I never even entertained the thought. The little that I did know about it disgusted me.

And I let her know how I felt about it without mincing my words because, right now, I really don't care about her feelings. She's grown enough to carry out foolishness like this and tell lies to manipulate friendships, then she's grown enough to hear exactly how I feel about the situation. I've been too nice for too long with her.

So now we have been arguing back and forth for a while, and I'm tired, sleepy, and mad as Hades and just ready to throw my phone (but I know better than that), so I just let her know that I'm tired of talking to her and that I just wanted her to get off my phone.

But by this time, she is really upset because I have called her on the carpet about her lies and told her how I feel about lesbianism and that if that's what she wants to do, then that's between her and God, but don't try to bring that foolishness up in my face and think I'm just gonna go with it. That there is nothing a woman can do for me but my hair! (No offense intended. I was just really trying to be mean right here.)

I was deliberately being mean, which is something I never do, but I was really upset. This is the part of me that even I don't like to see. I knew this wasn't normal for me. This wasn't my heart, but I needed her to hear my anger because, somewhere in my willingness to show her love and compassion, she decided to take advantage of it and twist it into something it wasn't. So I have nothing nice to say, nor do I want to say anything nice right now.

She kept trying to bring the conversation back to civil. That wasn't working at all. Civil was the last thing I was trying to be with this conversation. She would've been better off just hanging up and leaving me alone, because I wanted to say things to hurt her. Good thing I don't cuss because she would get an earful right now. I'm so mad I could cry. I want to just hang up on her, but I don't because I want to hurt her with my words. I want to be sure to say all that I want to say to her before I hang up on her, never to talk to her again.

I think she knew she had awakened a sleeping monster and probably never fathomed she would ever hear me speak to her in such a way. And she never would have had she not been so manipulating. I absolutely hated that this is where I was in my spirit, but I was and it was hard to turn it off. I did my best to hurt her feelings on purpose. If she was woman enough to go after grown women that she knew wasn't gay, then she was woman enough to deal with the consequences.

Then she began to cry. Man, I'm so mad right now, I really don't even care about her tears. She tried to talk through her tears and apologize for feeling the way she did and vowed to just go away. I told her that was the best thing she had said all night. I could tell that cut her deep and I wanted it to. She began to cry harder and was unable to respond to what I said. The next thing I know, I was listening to a dead phone. She'd hung up on me. "Good riddance," I shouted, "*YOU FREAKIN' LESBIAN!*" Don't ever call me again! I wanted to scream! (James 1:20: human anger...)

I got up and paced the floor, trying to calm myself down. I really needed to pray because to be this angry was not okay. I got on my knees and tried to talk to God, but all I could do was ask Him to help calm my spirit. I didn't want to be this angry. I stayed on my knees in prayer position just praying that God would honor my posture of humility because I couldn't really find the right words to pray with such anger in my heart. He knew why I was on my knees. He could hear my heart. The longer I stayed on my knees, I could feel Him calming my spirit. Little by little, I was getting back to being civilized.

I should've been praying for her, but truthfully, that was the last thing on my mind.

Still on my knees, I got to a place where my breathing had returned to almost normal. Normal enough for me to get up and get in the bed. I was tired, hurting, and angry. This did not go like I expected. I went from extreme anger to now I'm hurting. Why was I hurting though? Because I got out of character and allowed myself to go to a place where I didn't care about hurting someone else. Not only did I not care but I deliberately tried to hurt her. And I'm pretty sure I succeeded.

As tired as I was, I couldn't sleep because my mind was racing. Now I'm beginning to wonder if she is okay. As angry as I was, I knew I went too far with that last statement. Now I'm questioning myself, was all that really necessary?

"Come on, chick! That wasn't Christlike at all! But I was upset, I thought to myself. But that doesn't give you the right to disregard her feelings and not try to understand her struggle," my conscience responded. "She's already hurting because she didn't want to disappoint you. You didn't really even try to listen to her. You were cutting her off because you felt like what she was saying was irrelevant because she lied to you. So you felt like anything she had to say was null and void. Not fair, Nita, not fair at all."

All of a sudden, my feelings went from angry at her to angry at myself, because I knew she was hurting. I was pretty sure of it from the way she was crying on the phone and how she hung up on me. I'll bet that, just like me, she never thought this conversation would end up here. Now what? I couldn't just leave it like this, could I? Should I? Just let it go. What's done is done, right? Just go to sleep. She'll be fine, just check on her in the morning. This probably isn't the first time she's gone through something like this.

But I couldn't sleep. My mind was going a mile a minute. I was having bad thoughts cross my mind like her trying to kill herself because I made her feel so bad. Just horrible thoughts kept flooding my mind and I couldn't sleep as tired as I was. If she tried to harm herself, it would be all my fault because I spoke to her in such an awful and careless way. I began to think maybe I should just call her and check on her, but then something said no, just go to sleep. But when I tried, I couldn't.

I decided to at least just call her back and apologize for the terrible things I said and let her know that I will talk to her when I was more levelheaded but to just give me some time to think. I provoked her to hang up on me, so it was only right for me to call her back and apologize for my actions.

I found the strength and courage to call her back and apologize for the awful things I said because I said some really mean things. I called and her phone rang several times before going to voice mail. No problem. Maybe she's in the bathroom or something and missed my call. So I called again, and again, it went to voice mail. Wow! Well, maybe she's still crying and can't answer right now but if I call back, she'll know that I really need her to pick up the phone. Still no answer. Okay, I'll just call until she picks up. Still she doesn't pick up. No way, you've got to be kidding me! She's not gonna answer? Okay, fine, forget it then.

I lay back down to try to go to sleep but the thoughts of "what if" keeps flooding my mind. Now I really feel horrible, and I'm beginning to seriously worry about her.

Is she okay? Was I that rough that she would go and try to harm herself? Yes, I was pretty terrible, but I'm praying that she has more sense than to do something that stupid. I began to pray, "Lord, please don't let her do nothing crazy!"

I got up and called again, this time out of fear that she might harm herself. Still no answer. Now I was desperate. I really needed to know she was all right, so this time I left a message for her to please call me back and let me know that she was okay and that I was sorry for allowing myself to get so angry and say the mean things that I said.

I called again after I had left a message and again after that call.

Okay, well, I'm convinced she is not going to answer tonight, but I'm praying that it's not because she went and did anything foolish. God, have mercy on us both because if anything happened to her, how could I live with myself knowing how our last conversation went? Now my heart was hurting for her and worried about what I would have to face in the morning.

I was dead tired at this point, and it was about three in the morning. I wanted desperately to go to sleep but how was I supposed to with this on my heart? I'd just ripped this girl's poor heart to shreds with my irresponsible words, and now I don't know what's going on on her end because she either won't answer or can't answer the phone.

You'd better pray that she's okay because if not, you are going to be in a world of trouble.

Chapter 8
Wait... What Just Happened?

My eyes were burning. I was so tired. Ironically, after all the smack I had talked to make sure she knew how little I cared about her at that point, she had now become my main concern. I just wanted to make it right or right my wrong and be done with it. But she had stripped me of that privilege. As powerful as I thought I was telling her off, putting her down, and judging her, now I don't feel so powerful. She took it all by hanging up on me and not answering my calls. And now I'm so tired. I can barely hold my eyes open. I really need to go to sleep because tomorrow's the day we do the live taping for the comedy show. Wow! This is too much to be dealing with while I'm at this conference.

The best thing for me to do now is just go to sleep. There is nothing else I can do except pray and leave it in God's hands. I'm repenting for the things I said to her and praying for the opportunity to apologize. The Blood of Jesus keep us both.

In Jesus' name I pray, amen.

The next morning to my surprise, I woke up early, probably around 7:00 a.m., which was shocking because I didn't go to sleep until about 4:00 a.m. I couldn't really sleep with all that had transpired with Chloe. When I woke up this morning, I couldn't believe this was actually happening and had hoped for a moment that maybe it was just a dream. But it wasn't—it all really happened.

Then the disappointment in the way I acted last night cast a big shadow over me and I remembered I needed to call her. I know it's early and she's probably still asleep and the last thing she wants to do is talk to me, but I really got to know that she is okay and didn't do anything stupid last night.

Although I'm pretty sure she's not going to answer, but I have to call. The fear of what might be if she doesn't answer this morning is overwhelming. It makes me almost afraid of calling because I'm not sure I want to find out something is wrong. God have mercy on me, is my prayer.

I called her and waited as the phone rings on and on, and I'm thinking the worst because I know I'm about to get the voice mail. Either she hates me that much now and refuses to ever talk to me again or something is really wrong. Now I'm praying as the phone approaches its last few rings, "Father, please have mercy," and all of a sudden, she pick up and answers the phone.

I'm so relieved that I'm speechless and near tears. It took me a moment to respond, but I knew I couldn't take long or she would think I was still angry and calling to argue some more. "Praise God!" was my heart's cry. And for a moment, I was silent again because I was just thanking God that she was okay. It took me a moment to gather my thoughts and speak to her about why I was calling. When she answered, I could tell I had awakened her. Her "hello" was very low and a little fuzzy. I could tell she had been crying all night because she still sounded stuffy and snotty. By now, all I could think to say was "Hey, Chloe," almost as lightly as she spoke when she answered the phone. After another brief moment of silence, I mustered the courage to thank her for answering my call because I know she doesn't want to talk to me after all the mean things I said to her. I told her I wanted to apologize for the things that I said but that when she told me she loved me, it made me mad.

She said she understood and that it was probably too much too fast. I ignored that comment for the sake of keeping the peace. She went on to explain why she couldn't answer the phone on last night because she was hurting so bad from the things I'd already said to her and she couldn't take a chance on hearing anymore. She told me she was so distraught that her godmother (whom she lived with) came into the room to console her.

I apologized again and asked for her forgiveness for the way that I acted and the things that I said. I apologized for allowing myself to get so angry. She said she forgave me and that she kind of understood my anger but couldn't understand why I would say such mean things. She still sounded really sad. I expressed to her how worried she had me when she wouldn't answer the phone. She apologized for worrying me.

By now I was sitting up in the bed Indian style with the covers over my legs up to my waist. Although the conversation was going pretty slow and our voices were somber as we spoke very quietly to one another, almost straining to speak to each other as well as hear each other, we continued to force the conversation.

I could understand why she had reservations about talking to me now, but I wondered if she understood my reservations to speak to her. Not just because I felt weird because I know that she's attracted to me but also because I was ashamed of myself for the way I responded. Until now, I had probably done a fairly good job of being the Christlike example I should've been in her presence, but now I felt like it all went down the drain and she now looked at me differently aside from her attraction to me.

I could still hear the sadness in her voice when she spoke, and it would make me feel more ashamed. She apologized for falling in love with me. To hear her say those words cut me like a knife and rendered me speechless. How am I supposed to respond to that? My heart was still heavy as well. I was hurting for the both of us. This was a very unfamiliar place for me. I've had my heart broken and I've broken hearts and we've had these kinds of breakup conversations. But I've never been in this place with a woman! This was way too weird for me.

She began to cry again. It seemed as if she didn't want me to know she was crying so she tried to hide every sniffle and tried hard to control her breathing, but I could tell she was crying. My heart went out to her. I began to plead with her not to cry. But that seemed to make her cry harder in a way that she could no longer conceal it. She now was crying almost involuntarily, like she didn't want to but had no control at this point.

My heart broke for her. Why did she struggle with this? Why did she fall in love with me? She knows I'm not gay. Why would she let it get to this point knowing she didn't have a chance with me?

Her tears were breaking my heart. I really hate to see people hurting. And I really have a hard time dealing with the fact that I hurt someone. It just doesn't sit well with me.

I tried to console her as best I could over the phone. I was constantly telling her not to cry and that we would get through this. She told me I didn't have to try to be nice to her and that she knew I didn't want to continue to be her friend anymore.

I told her that wasn't true and that I wasn't going anywhere and that God would get us through this and we would be okay. She was still crying. Like the things that I was saying hurt her even more. Why?

I continued to plead with her not to cry. It really bothered me to hear her crying like this.

I was trying desperately to comfort her with my words. And before I knew it, I had said something I knew I shouldn't have said as soon as it came out of my mouth.

I remember as clear as day how weird I felt after I said it. Even in disbelief myself that something like that parted my lips. I told her, "If I were there, I would hold you, and I wouldn't let go until you told me to." Wow! Did I really just say that? Why?

I didn't regret saying it then, but I knew I shouldn't have said it. Something in me shifted. Everything in me disagreed with that statement, but I didn't take it back. I wanted her to be okay and to stop hurting. I think what I said was even a little shocking to her because she paused for a moment when I said it, and I think I even froze for a moment in disbelief.

She told me not to say things like that if I didn't mean it. Now, as if what I'd already said wasn't enough, I went on to say to her I did mean it and that I did want to hold her if it would make her feel better.

Now I'm concerned because I felt like I was flirting with her a little bit, and I didn't know why I was doing that. Why was I all of a sudden talking to her like this? Did I feel that guilty for hurting her? Did I feel like I owed her something? What was I doing? Just pray with her and hang up the phone—that would be wisdom. This was getting too weird.

At this point, I knew I'd gone too far, but for some reason, I didn't turn around and go back when I knew I should. What had come over me to make me think this kind of talk was okay? I don't play with fire like this. I don't think I was able to think rationally. This wasn't me. My main concern was making her feel better. But not by flirting with her! She's already in love with me. This was just going to lead her on even more!

After I said that, she seemed to cheer up a bit. Not to a point where she was smiling or laughing, but I could tell by her voice that she felt a little better, and at least, she had stopped crying. Well, if saying that to her made her feel a little better, then it was worth it, right?

Well, now that she was feeling a little better and we had been on the phone for a while, I let her know I had to go because I had a long day ahead of me and I had to get my head in the game but that I would call her back when I was done with everything later that day if that was okay with her. She said that was fine because she had some things she needed to get done as well. Her godmother came in the room to check on her while we were talking and I could hear her asking if she was okay, and Chloe assured her that she was and her godmother left the room. We commenced to saying our goodbyes and agreed to talk later.

We hung up, but as the day progressed, I could tell that something had gone horribly awry.

Something in me had shifted, and I felt it when I made the statement about holding her. Telling her I would talk to her later was not just to cheer her up or get her off the phone. As crazy as it sounds, I wanted to talk to her later and actually looked forward to it.

Wow! Where was all this coming from? This was crazy! Is this really happening?

After we hung up the phone, I got out of the bed to begin getting ready, but first, I got down on my knees to pray. I really needed to talk to God. I needed to hear from Him. Something was awfully wrong and I didn't understand what was happening. Was I really becoming attracted to her? Why? I'm not attracted to women! Why was this happening? God, please don't let this happen to me! I have no desire to be attracted to women at all! Father, please don't let the enemy do this to me!

As the day progressed and we were preparing to tape the live comedy show, the annoying feeling in my flesh grew ten times stronger and bothered me so much throughout the whole day that I began to cry. I had to go to a secluded place in the church we were doing the taping so no one could see me, but no matter what I did, that reeling in my flesh wouldn't leave me alone. It was so strong that it was scary. I had never felt anything like it before. The really strange thing was it felt good but annoying, and there was no reason for me to be feeling this way. The only times I've ever felt like this was when I was engaging in sexual acts with someone. Why was this going on in my body when I was just going about a normal day in my life. How was I supposed to do comedy feeling like this with all this stuff going on in my body? I was scared. I was crying and praying because I knew this wasn't normal and it wasn't okay. This was a spiritual attack from the enemy.

Chapter 9
Seduced

I knew nothing about spiritual attacks, absolutely nothing. So how did I know this was one? Because you don't just all of a sudden walk around feeling like you're going to have an orgasm for no reason at all. You don't just go from never having entertained a thought of being with another woman because the thought of it made you want to puke to now you can't wait to talk to her again overnight. And out of all the men I've loved and had relations with and as much as I love sex, I've never had currents run through my body for no reason at all. This definitely was not natural! This was a spiritual attack from the enemy. My question was, why? God, why? Little did I know, I would ask God this question what seemed like a thousand times before the year was over.

I had to get myself together so that I could go get makeup done. As much crying and praying as I had done, I was going to need plenty of it. I felt terrible going into this taping because I thought that because of the way I was feeling in my body, God would be angry at me for my sinful ways and not allow me to have a good set. I hated sinning against God, and I didn't take it well at all when I fell short. I walked nose-deep in condemnation, not realizing that it too was a sin.

I was grateful to get through the taping successfully and incredibly grateful to God for His mercy in spite of my failures and the way I was feeling in my body. None of this was making sense to me. I couldn't wait to get back to my room so that I could have a good cry and get it over with. I was able to put up a good front for the taping, but I was hurting. I was hurting deep on the inside and I couldn't explain it.

Allison and her daughter came to the show to support me, as did Minister Claudia. And as much as I looked forward to seeing them, I just didn't even want to be there anymore. I was just really ready for everything to be over. I wanted to go home. I was overwhelmed. This was too much, and I knew nothing about dealing with spiritual warfare, certainly not this kind.

My body was on fire, and thoughts of her flooded my mind. This was not okay. I was in a pickle. What do I do with this? I just needed to get back to my room because I was tired of acting like I was happy when I just wanted to cry. We all pretty much ate at the taping. They fed us pretty well there, with plenty to spare, so we took some back to our rooms for later. I talked to Allison and loved on her daughter a little before they left to go home. I knew I would see them for the weekend because we had already made plans to hang out. I spoke to Minister Claudia to let her know I really appreciated her coming out. When you know how busy people are and they make the sacrifice to come out, you don't take it for granted. It was truly a blessing to see her.

Once I got back to my room, I was looking forward to calling Chloe but I didn't want to do anything before I cried out to my Father. I was desperate to hear from Him. I was losing control and nothing made sense anymore. I got on my knees and began to cry out to God in a desperate way until I lay prostrate before Him in tears and a puddle of snot. (Yuck!) I needed Him to give me the strength to overcome whatever this was taunting me.

I needed to know He was with me and I pleaded with Him to not let me fall. What I was feeling was extremely strong, and I was beginning to feel helpless. I just didn't want to disappoint my Father by being weak. But I was weak and fighting a battle that I was completely unfamiliar with. I needed Jesus! I needed my Father to show Himself strong.

When I finished praying, I realized she had called while I was praying. I guess I was taking too long to call and it was getting late, so I guess she decided to take it upon herself to call me first. And seeing that I didn't answer, she left a message that seemed a little sad because she probably thinks I didn't answer because I changed my mind about talking to her. I texted her to let her know I would call her in a minute if she was still up. She texted me back that she was. I went into the bathroom to wash my face and get myself together. I called her once I got settled.

She asked me how did the taping go, and we had small talk about that. She told me that I sounded like I had been crying. I told her I had and that I had been crying most of the day. She asked me what was wrong. I told her "This! This is wrong!" and that now I was feeling like I was attracted to her too and that's not me and it's not what I want and I have no clue why I'm attracted to her.

"I'm not gay! And I'm not bisexual! And I'm not curious!" She chuckled a little bit, and I said to her, "It's not funny!"

She said, "I know, I know, and I don't mean to laugh, but you don't have to keep saying you're not gay. I know you're not gay."

I said, "So why would you allow yourself to fall in love with someone who you know is not gay? Why would you bring that to me?"

Then she dropped the old cliché: "You can't help who you love." I told her that was a lie from the pit of hell.

"People do it every day when we refuse the advances of someone else's husband or be sure not to show any interest in a man who is wearing a wedding band. Not because we wouldn't be attracted to him if he was single. He may be exactly what you were praying for, but because he's not single, he is someone's husband, he's off-limits! No if, ands, or buts about it. So that's not true. That's just an excuse for doing what you want to do."

"Okay," she said, "can we change the subject because I really don't want this to turn into another argument? I cannot go through what I went through last night."

I humbly apologized and let her know that what happened last night wouldn't happen again but that today was just really rough because I really don't know or understand what's happening to me right now. I told her that I believe I was under a spiritual attack, and she agreed that it very well could be what was happening.

Well, now the tables were turned. I was sad, and she was trying to console me. We talked until I was just too tired to stay up. It had been a really long day for more reasons than you can imagine. And it actually started the day before. So now I'm just exhausted. And I just want to go to sleep. She said she understood and that she hoped to hear from me tomorrow. I told her I would probably have to talk to her early in the day because Allison was coming to stay the night with me so we could spend some time together and then I would be at her house for the rest of the weekend but that I would be sure to give her a call sometime tomorrow. She told me that she hopes I feel better and that she would be praying for me. I thanked her, and we hung up.

    I cried myself to sleep.

Chapter 10
Transparent

The next day, I had gone through most of my morning just sitting and going through all that had transpired throughout the week in my head. I was really glad that I didn't bomb at the taping because I was dealing with so much that it was hard to focus. But praise be to God, he got me through it and I was so glad when it was over.

Overall, I have really enjoyed myself at the conference and was even given an award that I was totally not expecting for "best female stand-up Christian comedian." Although I think they were more so honoring my sacrifice to leave secular comedy and stay the course rather than me being deemed "the best." Either way, it was a beautiful glass plaque and truly a wonderful surprise. I was grateful.

Later that afternoon, I was still just kind of taken aback by all that had happened in just these past few days and just trying to make sense of it all. I was really sensitive in my spirit because every time I prayed, I cried. I just needed God to talk to me and tell me what was going on. Why was this happening? This made absolutely no sense. I was hurting, but I had to entertain company later when Allison would come to stay the night with me as we had planned, so I'd better get it together so as not to be a Debbie Downer. Allison and I usually had so much fun together. I could hardly wait till she would get here. I know she will cheer me up. Then I'm wrestling with who to confide in with this because I cannot deal with this alone. This is way too heavy for me, and I need someone to pray that I don't fail this test or whatever this is.

This is incredibly embarrassing and unbelievable that I would even have to tell someone that I'm feeling attracted to another woman. Utterly embarrassing. I am a woman of God. I'm not supposed to be here. Right?

Later that afternoon, I called to talk to Chloe. I knew she was waiting on me to call as I had promised her I would. It took me a while to do so because I was just in my feelings about everything that was going on. I was actually looking forward to talking to her but had reservations about calling because I knew in my spirit that I shouldn't. So it took me a while to call her, but I finally did and she was more than happy to hear from me. I could hear the smile in her voice. Our conversation was very pleasant toward one another, like we were on the same page. It was weird, but something about it felt good. It didn't matter though. Everything in me still screamed, "Wrong!"

I knew we shouldn't be talking, but now even the sound of her voice began to reel me in. The way she laughed and her level of maturity at such a young age had become so seductive to me and it was hard to tell her no. Everything was getting way too weird. I have never felt like this ever in my life!

We laughed and talked on the phone and had pretty normal conversation. Although I know she is attracted to me and I'm feeling some type of way about her, we didn't talk about that. Our conversation continued as it did before the attraction was revealed.

To me, that was a good thing. A sign that maybe we could push past this foolishness and salvage what I thought was a really cool friendship before this happened.

However, I did let her know that I believe in accountability, and that with everything that had transpired, there was no way I was going to try to get through this alone. I reiterated that I know it's an attack from the enemy. You can't explain this any other way. I've never in my life been attracted to another woman and all of a sudden this! I would be a fool to not think the enemy was behind all this. This was definitely the devil's work. I just didn't understand what I did to deserve to be here.

Don't ask me why I thought I had to deserve it for it to happen to me. The devil doesn't need a reason, but he does have to have permission from God when you're a child of God. And that's what I wanted to know. God, did you allow this? Why? What did I do? Was I a child of God's was never a question in my mind before, but I will admit that it did cross my mind when this started happening. It was shut down quickly though. I knew with everything in me who I was and whose I was, which only made this situation that much more baffling. I did my diligence to live my life holy and pleasing unto God, and this came out of left field and knocked me off my feet. I knew this wasn't me and that I didn't want no parts of this, and the best way to combat the enemy was to confess my faults to someone who could intercede for me and hold me accountable. I was willing to do whatever I needed to do to get this off me.

I let Chloe know that when Allison came that night that I was going to confide in her what was going on. I told her that I needed accountability and she did too and that she needed to find someone to talk to and let them know what she was dealing with.

She said she understood and that she agreed and would confide in her new best friend, Liz. We continued to talk for maybe another thirty minutes before hanging up so that I could get prepared for Allison to come later that evening.

Allison got to my hotel room around 7:30 p.m. We immediately went into girlfriend mode and began talking about our week and what got on our nerves and we talked about the conference and the comedy show. We talked about everything while we ate dinner we ordered from room service. While I was truly enjoying her company and had waited all week for this night with my friend, in the back of my mind, I pondered how to segue into what I needed to talk to her about. She was clueless to any part of that going on all week. But tonight, I would have to confide in her because I needed accountability and I needed to confess. There were many others I had considered before I decided on her, but they were either not saved or unable to counsel me correctly on something like this, or the fact that I just can't bring this to them; it's too embarrassing. I didn't know how Allison would respond, but based on the conversations we had had in the past, she seemed to be very mature spiritually. And we had hit it off really quickly and became so close so fast that I felt like she would be honest with me and hold me accountable accordingly.

Even though I'd only known her for a short period of time, I felt like I could trust her.

As the evening progressed, we had calmed the talking down and began to focus on TV.

My heart was beating so fast, I thought she would notice. I knew I had to muster up the courage to tell her what was going on.

It was getting late, and I knew we wouldn't be up much longer.

Ironically, she asked me about Sheila and Chloe and when was the last time I had talked to them. I told her that I had talked to Sheila earlier in the week but had not in the past few days and that I talk to Chloe pretty much every day. She was surprised to hear that we were talking every day. But she didn't make a big deal about it.

I thought this would be a good time to talk to her about what was going on. I told her that I needed to talk to her about something that was going on with Chloe. I told her earlier in the week how I discovered that Chloe was attracted to me. I told her that at first I tried to talk to her sensibly, but then she told me she was in love with me, and I lost it. How angry I got and some of the awful things I said to her. I told her she began to cry and eventually hung up on me. And after I thought about how I could've handled it differently, I tried to call back and apologize, but she wouldn't answer the phone. I got worried because I thought she might be so distraught that she might try to harm herself. I told her that I tried all night to no avail to contact her so I eventually just went to sleep. As soon as I woke up, I tried to call her again, praying she didn't do anything rash. I was relieved that she finally answered the phone. I apologized to her. She explained why she wouldn't answer the phone that night, and she apologized for falling in love with me. Then she started crying again. It was heartbreaking to hear her cry and so I tried to console her as best I could over the phone. Then I found myself saying something that was completely out of character for me, and as soon as I said it, I knew that I shouldn't have. But something shifted in me when I told her that if I were there, I would hold her until she told me to let her go.

She told me not to say things like that if I didn't mean it. I told her I did and that I would hold her if it would make her feel better.

Allison then asked me what made me say something like that to her. I told her I really don't know. I knew I shouldn't have said it as soon as I said it but I didn't even try to take it back. I told her that we talked a bit longer, but I had to get prepared for that day's events, and so we hung up cordially but not before I assured her that I would talk to her later. After giving Allison the story, I found myself trying to make sure that she understood that I'm not gay, I've never experienced anything like this in my life, I've never even considered such a thing, and that I am just as shocked about all of this as she is. I told her that I was telling her because I needed to confide in someone who would hold me accountable, because this was not me. And I was scared.

Before telling her, I never considered it could be too much too soon, or that she might think that I was always that way and this was my way of telling her. Maybe because we had spent countless hours on the phone since we met last October, and at this point, I don't think there is anything we don't know about each other.

But praise be to God, she believed me. Or at least she really seemed to. I had no reason to believe she didn't. I could tell she too was taken aback by the whole situation and she could see that I was hurting just from telling her the story, so she advised me to be really careful with Chloe. She said that she felt like this all may have been planned from the beginning.

I disagreed with her. In the beginning I thought so, but now not so much. She may not be completely innocent, but I don't think she did this on purpose. But Allison felt like Chloe knew what she was doing all along. She wasn't mad at me but I could tell that she now didn't really care for Chloe. Not that they ever really talked or anything, but they would say hello to each other if I was on the phone with one and the other was present.

I told Allison the same thing that I told Chloe, that I believed this was a spiritual attack from the enemy. She too agreed that it very well could be, but she would go on to say, "You better be careful with that young lady. I don't care what you say. She knew what she was doing."

After all was said and done, she agreed to hold me accountable and thanked me for confiding in her. She said she was sorry that I was going through this and that it would probably be a good idea not to talk to Chloe a lot. But to just be careful. I agreed with her completely and then we prayed. It had gotten really late and we both were dead tired and eventually just turned off the TV and went to sleep.

The next day when we got up, we went to breakfast in the hotel, and since that was my last day in the hotel, when we got finished with breakfast, we said our good byes to the comedians who were still there, then we went back to the room to pack my things to be out before checkout. Tonight I was staying at her house with her and her daughter for movie night, and I would go with them to church tomorrow before flying out to go back home.

It was a beautiful and sunny day although it was freezing cold. I had a great time hanging out with Allison taking me all over Nashville. I had come to love Nashville. I thought it was a beautiful city. A lot like Atlanta in many ways.

And I loved the mountains and the fact that it was cold when it was supposed to be cold and hot when it was supposed to be hot. I love when the seasons change. I don't want to live anywhere where it's hot most of the year or cold most of the year, not if I don't have to.

As the evening drew near and the sun was going down, we knew we needed to be heading back to her house. So we were driving to the store to pick up some snacks and a couple of movies. While we were riding, Chloe called, but I didn't answer. She left a message. Allison began to talk about what we had discussed the night before and reiterated once again, "I know that girl did that on purpose. I don't care what you say!" I just laughed and shook my head, and she chuckled too. When we pulled up to the store, Allison was about to run in real quick and get what we needed, and right before she got out of the car, my phone rang again. It was Chloe again. This time I answered. Allison stopped in her tracks and gave me a look like "Is that her?" I nodded my head yes. Allison then gave me the side-eye and mouthed "Be careful" and just shook her head and went into the store. She asked me what I was doing and I told her Allison and I were out and about but were stopping by the store to pick up some things before going back to her house for our "grown woman" sleepover.

She asked me if I got her message. I told her I hadn't checked it yet and was something wrong. She said no, she just wanted to talk. I then told her because tonight was our movie night and quality time with my friend, I was not going to be on the phone and that I, more than likely, would not be able to talk to her until I was on my way home at the airport tomorrow evening.

Although she sounded a bit disappointed, she said she understood and that she would wait to hear from me tomorrow evening. I said okay and we hung up. By the time Allison got back in the car, I was off the phone with her, so she gave me a bit of a lecture about talking to her and told me that I was going to have to stop talking to her as often as I did. I told her she was right and that I had plans to chill on the phone conversations. I appreciated her being frank with me and doing what I asked her to do and that was hold me accountable.

I really had a great time hanging out with Allison and her daughter. We called my daughter while we were all together and cut up on the phone with her for a bit. I enjoyed my time and fellowship with my friend. We stayed up late talking about everything and nothing. We were supposed to be having a movie night, but by the time we put the movie on, it was watching us because we all fell asleep. It was supposed to be a scary movie, but it was wack and we were worn-out anyway.

We all got up early and had breakfast before we went to church. After church, we came back to their house to eat dinner her mom had cooked for us. It was delicious. I was so grateful I got to spend quality time with her and her family.

Her parents were beautiful, godly people, especially her mom. And her daughter was like a niece to me. She even called me auntie. Shortly after dinner, it was time for Allison to drive me to the airport. I had a 6:00 p.m. flight and needed to be there at least an hour early to check in. So we left her house at three thirty.

On the way to the airport, Allison began to speak what had apparently been on her heart since Chloe called me when we were riding yesterday, but I guess she didn't want to dwell on it since we were having fun. But now was her opportunity to go in, I guess, because she spoke her mind and began to admonish me to walk away from the situation, or at least not talk to her as much. I listened to everything she said and I agreed wholeheartedly. But then while she was talking, this strong desire to talk to Chloe came over me. So I'm listening to my friend, but the whole time I can't wait to get to the airport so I can talk to her. I'm so conflicted right now I can't bring myself to tell her what I was feeling.

I had already planned to give her a call this evening when I was able to, but I didn't understand why now this strong desire to do so was so compelling, like it wasn't giving me a choice to. I had to call her when I got into the airport. And my body was now reeling again something terrible. I really didn't know what that was about. This was beginning to be a really scary situation.

We finally arrived at the airport, but I had gotten an earful on the way, and again, I could appreciate it because I was going to need someone who would be stern with me. As much as I wanted to tell Allison what I was feeling, I knew I needed to do so over the phone because this was going to take longer than either of us had to talk about it at the airport. I got out to get my bags and she got out with me. We gave each other a really tight hug. She is much shorter than me, so I had to bend down quite a bit to hug her. As always, we told each other we loved each other and she got in the car. But before she pulled off, she admonished me one more time to "be careful." I told her thank you and we smiled at each other and she drove off. I ran into the airport because it was still freezing outside.

Chapter 11
The Fight of My Life

Once I got in, I wanted desperately to call her but I knew I had to go through security so I texted her to let her know I would call once I got through security. Once I got through security, I decided I'd better call my mother and my daughter to let them know I was at the airport and try to make peace with my mom for not coming home for her birthday party. Of course, when I called, she was a little hot under the collar with me and told me I didn't love her because I would've come home for her party if I did. I let her know that my love for her was not contingent upon whether or not I drove home to be at her birthday party. That she knew I had a really busy weekend and would probably not make it. She fussed a little more, but we eventually kissed and made up like we always did. I told her I would make it up to her, and she let me off the hook. I love my mom, but she is a bit of a pickle. Afterward, I called my baby doll, my daughter, to let her know I was on my way home. She was so excited to hear it and couldn't wait for me to get there. The feeling was mutual. I really missed my little girl.

Now that I've talked to my best girls and made sure they were fine, I called Chloe. She was really happy to hear from me. Again, I could hear her smile through the phone. She asked me how our movie night went and told me she couldn't wait to talk to me and wanted to know if I talked to Allison about our situation. I told her that I told her everything.

She said, "Everything!"

I said, "Yes, everything."

I told her that there was no need for me to confess and ask for accountability if I wasn't going to be completely honest. I told her that yes, I'm feeling some type of way about you, but this is not me and I don't want this. I don't know why I'm feeling like this but I will do what I have to do to get past it.

"Okay, okay," she said. "I got it, I got it…" It was like she didn't really want to hear all of that. Then she asked me what did Allison say in response. I told her that she admonished me to walk away from this situation as a whole, and if I wasn't going to do that, then I needed to at least not talk to you so much. She asked what was my response. I told her I agreed.

"Oh!" she exclaimed with a chuckle. "So do we need to hang up now." She laughed.

I said, "Hey, if you want to hang up, we can hang up!"

"Whoa, whoa, whoa, whoa," she said, laughing. "I'm just playing, I'm just playing. Chill, relax… give me a few minutes!" We both just laughed.

I asked her if she talked to her friend Liz and what did she say. She said she did and that Liz pretty much said the same thing. Then she told me that Liz said she knew I was attracted to her before she told her. *EXCUSE ME! OH NO, MA'AM! SO NOT TRUE! THE DEVIL IS A LIAR! NO, MA'AM!*

"What would make her think that?" I asked. Why would she say something like that?

This whole thing has taken me completely off guard! "Why would she think that Chloe? What have you been telling her?" I was about to lose it up in the airport with this girl.

"Calm down, calm down, let me explain myself. Don't get yourself all worked up in the airport. Just calm down," she said.

"Girl, you better explain yourself quick because you know that's a lie yourself!"

Then Chloe began to explain that Liz said she had a dream and she saw this happening. Nah! No, ma'am, I've never felt an attraction to a woman ever in my life. I don't care what she dreamed! Why would she dream that about me?

"No, she knows you're not gay, but she just had a dream that this would happen," she said.

"Well, why didn't she warn you so that it wouldn't?"

Then she begins to chuckle at my obvious anger over her friend's somewhat epiphany. "It's not funny," I said. "This is not cool at all, Chloe! Both of you sound full of it right now! This is not okay and it's not funny!"

"Okay, okay," she said as she chuckled lightly. "Let's just talk about something else."

"I don't know," I said, "maybe we should just get off the phone. This isn't okay, Chloe."

"No, don't do that," she said. "I didn't mean to upset you."

"No, it's not just that. It's everything, Chloe. Allison and Liz are both right, and we shouldn't be talking to each other. Maybe we just need to go our separate ways. I'm feeling all crazy in my body and looking forward to talking to you on the phone... This isn't me! This ain't right, Chloe!"

She chuckled, saying, "You were looking forward to talking to me? Oh! "And what's going on with your body? Are you okay?"

"Yeah, it's nothing medical," I said. "I just feel really weird in my body, like a constant arousal."

"Oh, wow!" she said. "All this for little ole me?"

"Come on, really," I said. "Stop talking like that."

She couldn't help but laugh and I found myself chuckling too. By now I was walking up to my gate. Once I got there, I saw a lot of familiar faces, but most everybody was on their cell phones, as was I. I began to realize that it was a lot of Gospel artists flying home from the Stellar Awards. Some that I knew greeted me while I was on the phone and looking for a place to sit. I shared brief small talk with one of the singers that I knew, but she could tell that I was on the phone, so we hugged and said we'd talk when I got off the phone.

I found a seat and sat down and tried to resumed talking to Chloe as she was waiting for me to get settled because she could tell that I had run into some people and was waiting patiently for me to come back to the phone.

"So you see some people you know, huh?" She laughed. She had a Southern urban vernacular that came out strong sometimes when she was playing around and being loose with conversation. But most of the time she spoke very articulately. You could tell when she was giddy because the Southern urban twang was strong. She began to tease me a bit about how I was feeling in my body, asking me if I needed her to take care of that. *Clutch the pearls!* Did she just say that to me? She laughed, but I was seriously astounded… and aroused at the same time.

I said, "Heeeyyyy! You cannot talk to me like that!" But not in a way that was telling her not to talk to me like that. I was in utter disbelief that this was actually happening.

She continued flirting with me and saying things that had me blushing, smiling hard, and feeling crazy in my body at the same time. Was I really going to stay on the phone and entertain this? I was divorced and celibate for three years now, but was I that lonely or desperate that I would entertain this from a woman? Was this really happening?

She was flirting with me over the phone while I was in the airport and I was aroused. I had this feeling going on in my body for no apparent reason since the middle of the week and I couldn't figure out why I was feeling like this when I'd never experienced this before. And now she's on the phone flirting with me and teasing me and the feeling just escalated ten notches. God, help me!

And as much as I just want to get home, an announcement comes over the PA system that my flight was just delayed for another hour. *Really, people!*

When I told her what just happened, she laughed and said, "Well, I can stay on the phone with you until it's time to go." I could hear the ulterior motives in her voice.

I said, "No, that won't be necessary. We don't need to be on the phone much longer with the way you are talking to me and the way I'm feeling." I wasn't serious, and she knew it. We talked until my flight was about to take off and I had to hang up.

Once we landed, it was really late because of the delay and Nashville is an hour behind Atlanta. So I called my mother to let her know I had landed and was on my way home. She was in the bed, so we didn't talk long at all. Then I called my baby girl to let her know I was walking to my car and would be home soon.

I didn't call Chloe until I got to my car and was ready to roll. We talked until I got home, but I hung up before I went into the house. I needed to see my little girl who waited up for me. I wanted to get my hugs and kisses in and hear about her week and tell her a little bit about mine and the time I spent with Allison and her daughter. She couldn't wait to hear about my week and her sitter was preparing to leave, especially since I got back about two hours later than we had expected. But it is always a blessing to get home and find everyone blessed and in good spirits.

My sitter left, and my daughter and I stayed up for just a little while longer talking because she did have school the next day, and it was already past her bedtime. She already had her bath and gotten her pajamas on before I got home. So after we got caught up with each other's week, I walked her upstairs to her room and got her all tucked in bed, and it wasn't long before she was fast asleep.

I went and put my pajamas on and called Chloe back like I told her I would. It was now after 11:00 p.m. I had some stuff to do downstairs, so I was kind of preoccupied while we talked. I finally shut everything down and retreated upstairs. But instead of sleeping in my bedroom, I decided I would sleep in the guest room tonight, which was normally my prayer room. And I actually called it my throne room because this is where I really went in for worship, although I had a prayer closet in my bedroom.

Now I don't know why I would retreat to this room to continue talking to her because now the conversation was going way left. And even though I was enjoying it, I kept saying that we should probably hang up because I couldn't believe I was acting like that with a woman!

She didn't want to hang up and she continued to entice me with flattering and flirtatious words. As much as I wanted to get off the phone, I couldn't bring myself to hang up. Did I mention that her voice was very seductive? And as if that wasn't enough, she began to sing to me a song where the lyrics seemed very befitting to the situation at the moment called "Simple" by India Arie, whom at the time I'd never heard of. Or at least, I didn't realize I had. Turns out that I'd actually been on the same show with her two years earlier, but I didn't know who she was because I didn't listen to secular music at all. But as Chloe sang to me, the lyrics were beautiful, and she could actually sing a little bit. It made me feel a little bit better.

The longer we stayed on the phone, the more she would talk me into letting my guard down. I would do so until we got to a place of no return. This was too far. What was I doing? Why didn't I just hang up when I had a chance? Please tell me this is not happening? This shouldn't be happening even if it were a man because I'm not married, but it certainly shouldn't be happening with another *woman*! Have you lost your mind, girl? Did you seriously just do this?!

At this point, I felt so ashamed and I began to cry. As much as she tried, she couldn't get me to stop. Through my tears, I tried to explain to her that this was not me. It's not what I want. I am a woman of God, and I cannot be doing this. This is not okay!

My flesh was satisfied, but my spirit was deeply grieved.

By this time, it was five in the morning, and in about an hour and a half, I would have to get my daughter ready for school and I hadn't gotten a bit of sleep and I'm still in tears.

Ironically, she began to sing to me again another song by India Arie called "Beautiful Surprise." Again, I didn't know the song, but the lyrics were befitting. I managed to calm down a bit and stop crying so much, but I'm still hurting and all kinds of disappointed in myself, not to mention this utter disbelief that this just happened over the phone with a woman. A *woman*!

I feel like God must think the worst of me. How could someone who is supposed to be so in love with God allow such behavior in their life? I had reached an incredible low—a low I had never considered, not even once when I was in the world. How did I get here as a woman of God?

This was way too much for me to deal with any further tonight. I can barely breathe from the snotty nose I got from crying. My head is hurting. My heart is broken. I'm dead tired, and I just want to go to sleep. She agreed, and we finally hung up.

I didn't know what I had just gotten myself into, but this is where I would begin the fight of my life. From that day forward, everything was different. Nothing would ever be the same again. My heart was broken because I just didn't handle failure well.

Not only that, I just really didn't understand how this was happening.

Where did this come from all of a sudden that I would allow myself to entertain something that I honestly thought was so vile and disgusting.

I would think that if this was something that I had lying dormant and just hadn't dealt with, there would've been something in me that gave me a clue. Something I could reach back to and say, this is why you felt this way or acted that way in this situation, but God as my witness, I honestly don't. I got nothing to go back to that helps me understand why I'm here.

I got up and got my daughter off to school, feeling like death warmed over. I couldn't wait to get back home and get some real sleep. But once I got home, sleep was the last thing on my mind. I went into my prayer closet and got down on my knees and cried out to my Father. I wept with everything in me until I had nothing left. Then I fell asleep in my prayer closet, really uncomfortable but too broken in my spirit to move.

About three hours later, I got up and got in the shower. Afterward, I lay down in my own bed, trying desperately to get some sleep before I had to pick my daughter up.

Shortly after dozing back off to sleep, my phone rang. I answered without looking. It was Chloe. She apologized for waking me. I told her it was okay. (It wasn't really.)

She asked me how I was doing, and I told her, "Horrible." I told her this is not me and that it couldn't happen again. She told me she would go away and I agreed... again.

I apologized to her a thousand times because I knew it hurt her to hear me say that I agree to her going away. I felt terrible that I wasn't strong enough to resist her advances, thus ruining our friendship. I'm much older, so I felt more responsible.

I should've said no and shut it down from the very onset. If I hadn't entertained her flirting with me, she would've never thought this was okay.

Chapter 12
I Do What I Hate

Now I've gotten myself in a situation that would prove to be far from easy to get out of.

From that day forward, for the next several months, I would be on an emotional roller coaster with this young lady, fighting to get my life back in order with God.

The enemy was strategic and crafty through her. No matter how much she said she would go away, she wouldn't go away. She would always worm her way back into my life one way or another.

Allison, by this time, was perturbed with the whole situation, and it was beginning to cause friction with our friendship. Although by this time she wasn't the only one I had confided in. I went to my pastor in Knoxville, Tennessee, and I told him everything from the beginning to where I was now. I told him that I've never been attracted to another woman in my life and that I was just as baffled as anyone could be about this situation. I told him the truth about how I felt about her and how I was hurting because this wasn't me. I told him I needed to let him know so he could intercede for me and hold me accountable. That if I kept it a secret, the enemy would run amok with it.

He knew it had to be embarrassing to have to tell him something like this because he knew I was diligent to live a holy life, to a point where I'm sure I got on his nerves with some of my legalistic ways. (I didn't realize then that I was being legalistic.)

He talked to me in love and confirmed what I already knew and that was that this was a spiritual attack. That the enemy wanted to destroy my testimony. (I didn't think about that.)

He reminded me of the story of Joseph and Potiphar's wife and how, when she tried to entice him, he did everything he could to get away from her, thus leaving his garment behind as she pulled him by it, and he came out of it to get free from her. Pastor told me to do whatever I had to do to get away from her.

As we talked a while longer, I began to cry because I just didn't understand how I was tangled up in something I had no desire for. It made no sense to me at all, and it was the worst feeling in the world. I've never experienced anything like this before. I have sinned and regretted it and repented. But it was more than likely something I wanted to do even if I didn't want to do it because I knew it was a sin and it was wrong to sin against God. But I did it because I wanted to and I knew I would enjoy it. And I may have felt terrible afterward and full of regret for my sins, but a part of me wanted it because, for some reason, I desired it.

This is not the case here. I have no desire to be with another woman, and I don't want this. So why am I entertaining something I DON'T WANT!

Before we got off the phone, Pastor prayed for me and told me that he would call to check on me. I felt a lot better after talking to him even though it was really embarrassing to have to tell him that.

When Chloe called me again, I only answered to let her know that we couldn't talk anymore. But I wish I had just not answered the phone. Why I felt the need to tell her that is beyond me because she hadn't listened the other hundred times I had already told her.

I told her I had talked to Pastor Aye, and I suggested that she talk to him too, because even though he told me to run from this situation as fast as I could, he was concerned about her soul as well. I too had tried to minister to her, praying with her over the phone, and I think she only listened to appease me for the moment because she always went back to the shenanigans a little while afterward.

She was angry with me for telling Pastor Aye, but I knew not telling him would only benefit her. I needed more accountability because Allison had pretty much abandoned me by this time. I think she tried to do her part to hold me accountable, but it just proved to be too much for her. I was honest with her about everything. I never lied to her, and I think it was my truths that she couldn't handle. I think it got to a place where she didn't believe I wasn't gay. I think she felt like I wanted to be where I was. She had no idea the pain I was in and how I was tormented in my spirit over all of this. I knew I was losing her and it really hurt because I loved our friendship and I loved her and her family. I thought she was strong enough to help me through this, but I realized it was too much, and it wasn't what she signed up for. Losing her friendship was heartbreaking. But what hurt even more was the fact that she didn't believe me. I could tell she was no longer interested in our friendship, so I let her go and we went our separate ways. Man, that hurt!

But as for Chloe and her new "best friend," their friendship was thriving. I don't know what Chloe was telling her about me, but for some reason, she really didn't like me. She was a year younger than Chloe but full of wisdom, even more than Chloe. I think that's why Chloe adored her so because she was very mature for her age.

Liz had a heart to serve the Lord and did so with diligence. She knew Chloe's past (and present), but I guess she felt safe because she knew Chloe liked older women. It seemed that in her eyes, Chloe could do no wrong. She always took everything Chloe said at face value, never willing to hear the other side of the story (or what I had to say about what was going on). "But she's full of wisdom," you say. I know and she is. She just missed the mark on that part.

I always wanted desperately to apologize to her for my failures and the fact that she had to cover me while all this was going on. She didn't have to, but she chose to, and I praise God for that. That's part of the wisdom and maturity I was talking about. But she refused to talk to me about the matter. I could never understand her disdain for me when she had never talked to me about any of this or heard my side to know that I didn't want this. Little did she know that unbeknown to her or Chloe, God would use her inadvertently, in this whole process (to help me).

I was my biggest hindrance in this situation because of my inability to just walk away, close and lock the door, and throw away the key.

Chapter 13
The Longer You Stay

There were times I would have to be stern with Chloe to get her to go away. And then there were times when I had to be downright mean to make her understand that I didn't want this. I was so miserable and pitiful that I cried all the time, pleading with her for this to just be over, so much so that I really couldn't understand why she put up with me. Why she even wanted to. Why not just move on to someone who wants you like you want them? She knew I hated this. Why wouldn't she respect my wishes and just go away, and stay away! I knew I had to find a way to get free from her soon because the longer I stayed would only make it harder to overcome.

I was miserable. But the truth of the matter was, I had fallen for her too. She was very seductive, and she had this sweet voice and a way about her that just melted my heart. It was hard to be mean to her and hard to deny her, which is another reason I knew it was a demonic spirit. She was pretty but she wasn't drop-dead gorgeous. I don't say that to be mean. I say that to say that I have seen (and still see) some incredibly gorgeous women throughout my lifetime, but I have never seen one that I was attracted to in the least! Not a single one! Not in real life or on TV! Moreover (and God knows I'm not trying to be mean, I'm trying to make a point), I don't think I would've been attracted to her if I was gay. For one, she was much younger than me. I don't even like my men to be younger than me, certainly not seventeen years younger!

Which brings me to another point. I realized that as much as I felt for her and all these unfamiliar feelings I had for her, I was not attracted to other women. Now, trust me. I was grateful for that! But that was really strange to me because if this was something lying dormant that had come to be revealed and awakened, shouldn't I have been attracted to other women too? I'm asking for a friend because I'm sure some of mine are worried that they might have been sized up. Please don't be. I assure all of you that you were never in any danger of being hit on!

My compassion for her made it hard for me to walk away and stay because I knew how bad it would hurt her, and I hated hurting her. (I hate hurting anybody.) And she made sure I knew she was hurting. But this was killing me, and she knew it. She didn't care as long as she got what she wanted. She was kind of selfish like that.

I valued what I thought was a good friendship between us. I could talk to her about anything and she was a good listener (a lost art today). She was witty like myself, so we had a lot of fun on the phone most of the time. We laughed together a lot and had really silly conversations. It was hard to believe we had seventeen years between the two of us. I would impart wisdom to her when she was dealing with certain situations, and she would help me understand this new technology better. She was really good with computers and stuff. Millennials! She was always there to talk to me when I was having a bad day or needed to cry or just going through for reasons other than us.

She would even check on me when I traveled, asking me how my show went and allowing me to elaborate. She would call during her lunch breaks and talk to me about things that bothered her. She trusted me with her heart. She loved me and it felt good to be loved. Basically, she did everything I wanted in my man. But isn't that's just how the enemy does it? He sets it up just the way you like it (except he missed the most important factor—I like *MEN*).

I enjoyed her company in my life. I enjoyed our friendship. I just didn't want her to be attracted to me and I didn't want to be attracted to her. That was the part that hurt the most because we had such a cool friendship, and I knew in order to get through this, I had to let everything go. I didn't want to be in a relationship with a woman. But it wouldn't be enough to just kill the attraction. The friendship had to die too. And that was my biggest struggle.

But she wanted to have it all. She wanted a relationship, and I wasn't about to be in a relationship with a woman. As much as we laughed and cut up at times, we also fought just as much. That's what happens when you're not on one accord, and we were not. She told Liz that we argued every day. That wasn't true. I wouldn't entertain anyone's company that I argued with every day. There were things we enjoyed about each other, but I didn't want what she wanted and she knew that, because I constantly let her know. She also had a short fuse, a bad temper. It didn't take much to set her off. So it was a good thing we lived hours away from each other for more reasons than one.

She would curse at me when she was upset, knowing I hated when she used profanity with me. It was disrespectful.

Sheila still called me as well, and we all knew that we all talked. But Sheila had no clue this was going on between us. And even though they were childhood friends, Sheila was also clueless that Chloe was a lesbian. Chloe was apparently quite good at keeping her lifestyle secret because her parents nor her siblings knew. There would be times when I would beg her to just talk to her mom about it so that she would know how to pray for her. Her parents were Christians and they seemed to have a good relationship. I just couldn't imagine them not loving her through it. But she wouldn't even think about going to her parents about it. I would plead with her to talk to my pastor in Knoxville and that we could talk to him together but she wasn't having it.

Pastor Aye would call and check on me to see what was going on. And no matter how bad the report, I was always honest with him. I hated having to tell him that she and I were still communicating when he had admonished me to get out of there. And I tried desperately to do everything he asked me to do. I tried so many times to just shut it down. She just wouldn't go away.

I remember being in Knoxville for an event for Pastor Aye, and he met my daughter and I at the hotel because he wanted to talk to me and pray for me in person before the event. We met in the lobby and began to talk, but then I was a bit overcome with emotion, and we decided to just go to the room so he could pray for me.

We both knelt by the bed while my daughter sat in the living room watching TV.

As he prayed for me, I wept bitterly. I know his heart broke for me. I know that he knew that I didn't want this. He knew I wanted out. He continued to pray earnestly for me and I wept so hard that I began to sweat and my face was drenched with tears as I buried it in the beautiful white comforter on the bed where we knelt. When Pastor was finally finished praying, we both got off our knees only to find that the place where my face was, was completely bloodied. I didn't realize that I had wept so hard that my nose began to bleed. I had ruined this gorgeous white comforter. I was very apologetic but Pastor explained to me that God was reminding me of the blood of Jesus Christ over my life. Praise God! (But somebody's gotta pay for this comforter!)

After Pastor had prayed and laid hands on me and declared the victory over my life from this demonic attack, I was relieved and I felt victorious in my spirit. When my daughter and I returned home after the event, I was actually able to lay down the law with Chloe and shut some things down. I told her this had to end here and now. We cried together and decided to go our separate ways. She didn't bother me after that, for three whole days. On the third day, I got an e-mail from her. I didn't answer back. Then she called the same day. I didn't answer. She called again. I didn't answer. She called again, I answered. She was hurting. She just needed to hear my voice she said. We talked and I tried to comfort her, but I let her know that we could not carry on like we did on the phone anymore. If it happened again, I was gone for good. She agreed. She would behave.

We actually began to have civil conversations and kept the foolishness at bay. When she would try to go left, I would reel us back in. We were keeping our word and it felt good because it felt like we could get through this and remain friends. And that's what I wanted because I thought we had a really cool friendship.

This had gone on for a couple of weeks, and there was a big conference coming to Atlanta that she'd gotten VIP tickets to at the last minute and wanted to know if I would go with her. I actually really wanted to go to the conference, but I hadn't gotten my ticket yet. So it was cool that she had free tickets. And VIP at that!

She drove up from Jacksonville and met me at my house because the conference didn't start until later that evening. When she got to my house, for some reason, she parked in front of my house instead of in the driveway. This would be my first time seeing her in person since Gainesville, Florida. When she got to my house, I already had my shower and I was dressed but not in what I was wearing to the conference because I was curling my hair when the doorbell rang. My heart was racing when I went to answer the door. I was really nervous to be seeing her in person again—for obvious reasons.

When I opened the door, we both were smiling way too hard. I kind of hung my head and turned and opened the door wider and backed up so she could come in. I was too ashamed to look at her so we were both giddy about it. She asked me why couldn't I look at her, and I could hardly speak. She chuckled. I was really nervous about seeing her, but I didn't think I would respond like this. She treated me like I was the little girl. I gave her a quick hug, but I just couldn't look at her. Too much had transpired over the phone and we had done things that now made me ashamed to face her.

As we stood in the foyer, she came close to me and got in my face, but I backed up and turned my back to her. She then softly walked up behind me and put her arms around my waist as she stood close to me trying to get me to turn around. I would not, so she began to talk softly to me while we stood there with her holding me from behind. Before I knew it, she kissed me on my neck. I couldn't believe it. I froze. She asked me to turn around so she could see me but I just couldn't. She then came around to stand face-to-face with me and asked me to look at her. It took everything in me to do it, but I lifted my head to look at her. We were about the same height. She was maybe an inch shorter. Again, before I knew it, she had kissed me softly on my mouth. My knees buckled because I couldn't believe she touched my mouth with her lips. I had just been kissed on the mouth by a woman!

I allowed her to come and visit me because my daughter was

visiting with my family in North Carolina for spring break and I thought we had gotten to a place in our friendship where we could be around each other and just be friends. Besides, we were going to a church conference. Obviously, I was grossly mistaken.

Needless to say, we didn't make it to the conference that night or any night that week. She stayed at my house with me for about three days. I had to leave for an event in Chattanooga, Tennessee, that weekend, so she had to leave too. But after all that had happened, I was ready for her to go because I was grieving in my spirit something terrible. And I had to walk around like I was okay in front of her, and I wasn't.

I was hurt, I was angry, I was sad, and a whole plethora of emotions that I was experiencing.

I was in disbelief that it actually went that far. I was mad that it felt good. I was mad that I was foolish enough to think we would be okay. I was mad that I ever met her. I was mad that I was so weak. But more than anything, I was mad that I had failed God.

I felt an incredible brokenness. It was an indescribable, gut-wrenching pain that was constant. I hurt from the depths of my entire soul. What had I done? How much worse could this get? How much worse would this get? I've made some really bad mistakes in my life, but this was lower than my lowest.

I'm waiting on her to finally leave because I desperately need to go pray and cry out to God and repent for my sins. I'm even embarrassed to bring this to Him, but I know that I have to. As foolish as this was, I knew it would be even more foolish not to pray and repent.

I know she could tell that I was hurting, as much as I tried to hide it. I don't know why I felt like I had to hide my feelings. Maybe because we both had to get on the road, and I needed her to leave and not try to stay and console me. On top of all this mess, I had an event that I had to do tonight. How was I supposed to minister like this? I was a mess! I'm hurting something terrible, not to mention how unworthy I feel to be on anybody's stage doing Christian comedy. Why would God give me His blessing to do well and be funny after I've fallen so low?

It was normal for me to walk in condemnation after a known failure. And the greater the failure, the greater the condemnation. And this was colossal! I really blew it this time!

Don't get me wrong. I knew that I served a forgiving God. That wasn't what I was worried about. I knew I would be forgiven, but I was more concerned about the consequences I would have to face! The uncertainty of what could come was unsettling. Now I needed to know my Father's heart concerning me. I knew I had grieved my Father. I had professed my love to Him a hundred thousand times. How, for God I live and for God I die. How He was my first and foremost. He was and is my heart's greatest desire. And nothing meant more to me than pleasing my Father. And here I was in a situation I couldn't bring myself to walk away from, and now it has led to the unthinkable. The pain in my heart was unbearable and I cried almost all the way to Chattanooga. It always hurt me deeply to sin against God. But this... this had me broken.

I got to my hotel room about two hours before show time, and I knew I had to pull it together. Of course Chloe had called while we were both driving. We only talked briefly because she understood that I wasn't in the mood for conversation and we would have to talk later. I was always nervous before a show, but today, I was petrified because God had no reason to give me His blessings, was how I thought. This could go really bad.

On top of that, I got a call from Pastor Aye. He actually lived in Chattanooga but pastored a church in Knoxville. He had called to check on me, and my goodness, this was not the time to tell him what had happened as much as I wanted to.

I just couldn't deal with all that before a show. I was way too fragile and would've been a crying shame for the rest of the night. I knew I had to wait to tell him. He asked me where my show was in Chattanooga because he might be able to come. I told him where, hoping he wouldn't make it. I just couldn't handle all of that right now. I needed to focus on getting through this event, and if I was going to bomb, I sure didn't need him to be there to witness it.

The promoter had all the artists picked up from the hotel and brought to the venue in a limo. It was really good to see some of the comedians because we didn't really work together anymore because of me making the switch from secular to Christian comedy. I started with these guys. So it was great to see them, but this wasn't a Christian comedy show. And I was the headliner.

It wasn't sold out, but it was a really good crowd. Everyone did really well, especially the girl who went on before me. I always thought her comedy was really clever and intelligent. Most people thought she acted too much like me onstage. To me, she was nothing like me. She had her own wit and I always knew she would do well. So I wasn't surprised that she ripped. I was just disappointed! LOL! Aside from me feeling like a pile of dung, now as the headliner, I had to top that! But I couldn't be mad at her; it wasn't her fault. She had nothing to do with what was going on between me and God and my indiscretions. This was all on me.

So then the emcee introduces me after she has ripped the stage and I go out to do what I do, knowing what I've done. Yes, it had to go onstage with me in the back of my mind.

And as if that wasn't bad enough, you stand onstage wondering if they can tell what you did last night. Ugh! The torment!

Unfortunately, this was nowhere near the first time I've had to grace the stage with a heavy heart (thanks to my two ex-husbands). Many times, life has come at me hard, and I had to walk right out there and do my job, make people laugh. God always got me through it. And although I broke His heart this week, He would still come through for me and let me shine as if though I had been his faithful servant (His mercy). For that I was grateful, but it made me feel even more unworthy. For this, I was all the more broken.

When the show was over, I discovered that Pastor Aye actually made it to the show. He came to the stage to let me know he was there. He wanted to check on me, and so I decided that I would ride with him instead of going with the other comedians to get something to eat in the limo. I wasn't really hungry and didn't feel like being around anybody (Pastor included), so I just packed up some of the food they had in the green room and took it with me so I could eat it once I got to my room.

Pastor Aye took me back to the hotel, and as soon as we got there, it began to pour down raining. He began to talk about how well the show went and that it was good to see me and that he thought me and the girl before me were the funniest. Of course he would say that to me, I thought. Truthfully, I thought she had the best set of the night, period. But I certainly would not complain considering my situation and the mercy God showed me in spite of me.

We sat in the car in front of the hotel and talked for a while before he finally brought up my situation with Chloe. Unlike any other time I would talk to him about it, I wasn't completely honest. After he asked me did we still talk and I told him yes, he would go on to basically lecture me about having to let it go or I would find myself wishing I had and how bad this could end up being. Little did he know, I was already there.

I wanted so desperately to tell him of my failures. The rain was pouring and beating against the windshield and the windows and I wanted to cry hard like the rain so badly.

I love Pastor Aye, and I think he is an incredible man of God who genuinely cares about his sheep. I think he's doing a great job of holding me accountable and I didn't want him to stop. But tonight, for some reason, I just cannot bring myself to tell him of my failure.

I think I even stalled our conversations, hoping I would somehow come up with the courage to tell him before he leaves. But it never came. And by this time, I was emotionally exhausted in my spirit, so he prayed for me, told me I did a great job onstage and that he was proud of me for how I handled the heckler. I laughed in spite of myself and got out of the car and he drove off. I couldn't wait to get to my room so I could talk to God.

But I really wanted to hear from Him. I got down on my knees to commune with God, but all I could really do was cry and repent. I was broken something terrible. But I was also grateful that God didn't embarrass me as he could have. I'm sorry, I know God is not petty and cruel, but I just don't take stuff like that for granted. I was overwhelmed to know that, in spite of my failures, God still saw fit to use me. And He didn't have to.

Chloe had texted me earlier that evening to let me know she had made it safely home. I was grateful but didn't want to talk to her that night. So I told her that I would give her a call when I got on the road the next day.

I checked out of the hotel the next day and stopped to get something fast to eat because I was hungry from not eating the night before. After I finished eating, I called Chloe as I had promised her I would. My mood was somber, and she knew I was unhappy with what happened between us at my house. She was probably confused because even though I cried right after it happened the first night, I was okay while she was there for the next two days (or so it seemed) until it was time to go. Then the severity of what had taken place really kicked in and knocked me back into reality. None of this was okay, but because I didn't run away like Pastor had admonished me to and just let her deal with her feelings, now I'm in over my head. Because I was so worried about hurting her feelings that I failed to take heed to what Pastor Aye and Allison told me to do and that was run, regardless of her feelings. But it just wasn't that easy for me.

I remember talking to her one day after I was trying to break it off and she was really sad and it really hurt me to hear the sadness in her voice, but something was strange about the way she was acting while we talked. I knew she was hurting, but she was too calm, and that wasn't normal when she wasn't getting what she wanted. I told you before she was a hothead. She had a temper. But while we talked and I explained that I didn't want this and I couldn't stay, she would simply say, "Okay, I understand… You gotta do what you gotta do, and so do I."

I asked her what that meant. What did she plan on doing? She just kept saying, "You'll see." I felt like she was trying to hint that she would come after me and now she knew where I lived. So I told her not to be trying to threaten me because I don't play those kinds of games and that she would wind up getting herself hurt trying to mess with me like that. She said she had no intentions of trying to harm me and wasn't interested in making idle threats. She was too calm, something wasn't right.

I asked her where was she, thinking maybe she couldn't talk like she wanted to because someone was around her. She said she was in the car. I asked her where she was going. She said nowhere. I asked her why she was just sitting in the car if she wasn't going anywhere. She said she was just ready to go.

I said, "Where are you going?"

She repeated that she was just ready to go. Now I knew something was wrong. I asked her where she was parked and she said in the garage. "So you are sitting in the car in the garage?"

Yes.

"Is the car running?"

Yes.

"Is the garage door open?"

No.

"Are you serious? What are you doing?"

"I'm just ready to go," she said just as calmly.

Now I was frantic because this girl was trying to commit suicide and I was nowhere near her to get to her. All I could do was plead with her, "Please don't do this! Please turn the car off, please!"

"No," she said, "I'm hurting, and I'm just ready to go."

I was about to lose it because I had to find some way to get her to turn her car off and not do this, but how? I was hundreds of miles away, and I didn't know anyone who lived near her to call. As a matter of fact, I didn't even know where she lived! I was in a pickle! If anything happened to her, that blood was on my hands! God, please help me!

Please don't let her do this! I continued to plead with her to turn the car off, and I was near tears. Then I began to think to call the police. Maybe they could find her and get to her before it's too late. I let her know that I was going to call the police. She told me it didn't matter that she was ready to go. I was scared to hang up because I was worried she may not pick up when I called back or if she would be able to. I continued to threaten to call the police and was near tears because all I could think of was how this would play out and I would be the culprit. Finally, she decided to turn the car off and sarcastically asked me was I happy.

"Are you serious! What is wrong with you? Why would you do that?" I then told her to give me something that assured me she turned the car off. I ask her to let me hear the garage going up and she did. "Let me hear you get out of the car and go outside. I need to hear you walking." She did, and I sighed in relief.

I had to wonder what had I gotten myself into with this girl. This was crazy!

I talked to her for a while longer that night just to make sure she would be okay. Me leaving wasn't a part of that discussion anymore because I really needed her to be okay.

Before we finally hung up, I told her I would check on her tomorrow. And we said our goodbyes.

The next day when I checked on her, she seemed to be in better spirits. I told her that what she did was not okay and had me scared to death and that nothing on this earth is worth taking your life for. Her response was, "Yeah, that wouldn't have been a good look for you, huh?" Then I began to think, *Wow, what in the world am I dealing with?*

I was relieved to get home from Chattanooga and get by myself for a minute. I didn't have to go pick my daughter up until the next day. I needed to be alone because I was in pain and I just needed the solitude. I was really disappointed in myself for not being able to tell Pastor Aye that she had come to visit me and things had gotten physical. I was even more disappointed that this was now my truth. I know I have to tell him. I think it was just way too embarrassing to do face-to-face. I'm not sure why I couldn't that night. I just knew I couldn't.

Ironically, Pastor called a few hours after I had gotten home to make sure I got in safely because I was supposed to let him know when I made it home but I forgot to. I thought maybe he had sensed that something was wrong last night, that I failed to tell him everything. But that wasn't it because he was a little too chipper when I answered, asking me if I was at home and wasn't I supposed to call him when I got in. I apologized for not doing what I was supposed to do, and I guess I wasn't as chipper as he was, so he asked me if I was okay. I told him I was not. He asked me what was wrong and was my daughter okay.

"Yes, Pastor, she's fine. It's me."

"What's wrong?"

"Give me a minute," I said, because I knew I couldn't just start talking or I would cry, so there was a long pause before I spoke. "Chinnita, what's wrong?" he asked.

In spite of my long pause, I couldn't hold back my tears. I tried to calm down so that I could get it out. He waited patiently for me to tell him what was wrong. Then he asked, "Is it that girl?"

I said yes. He said, "What happened?"

I told him as I wept that I slept with her. All I heard from him was a big sigh, and I knew he was greatly disappointed in me. He had every reason to be. He told me everything I needed to do, and as much as I tried to, I failed. He asked me when did all of this happen and I told him just before I came to the show she had left my house after staying with me for three days. I told him she had gotten tickets to go to the conference and she drove down so we could go together but we didn't make it to the conference.

I knew he was angry, because he said he was, but he said I was already hurting too bad for him to fuss at me. This threw me because I wanted to be rebuked and told what a hypocrite I was. I wanted a tongue lashing and I expected it. But that's not what happened. And I didn't understand it. I knew he was disappointed, and I knew he was angry and tired of my foolishness but that's not the emotion he displayed. I was perplexed by his mercy and kindness toward me. I was sick of me. I know he had to be. But he was patient and full of grace.

He talked to me and tried to calm me down from crying and told me we would get through this and that I was going to be all right. He thanked me for telling him. I told him that I wanted so badly to tell him last night, but for some reason, I just couldn't muster up the courage to.

He then said he had an assignment for me that he wanted me to do. That he was dealing with another situation like mine in the fact that this person knows she's not gay, but she was suddenly overcome with these feelings once a friend of hers began to come on to her. She too confided this in Pastor on her own. And he wanted us to talk because we kind of needed each other at this point for accountability.

I couldn't believe what I was hearing. For one, I always felt like if something like this was all of a sudden happening to me, someone who was never attracted to other women, how many other people has this happened to that were just too embarrassed to ask for help or just began to believe that they were gay and went with it. Because when all this happened, I did something I'd never done before, I questioned my sexuality! Fortunately, I was pretty sure about what I liked and what I wanted and didn't want. So the enemy tried to confuse me, but when you know what you know, you can't unknow it.

So I was pretty taken aback to hear that someone else in "the church" was dealing with this. But not shocked.

But then too I was blessed to know that he still trusted me to put someone else in my path to help them. At this point, I wasn't sure I could trust myself because I was doing things I never thought I was capable of. But he let me know, by doing this, he believed me and he believed in me. This blessed me incredibly, although I felt too unworthy to be able to help anyone. But it was worth a try.

He gave her my number, and a few days later, she called me. Her name was Nyla. We talked for a long time that day, explaining our situations to one another. I think we even cried a few times, trying to understand what and why this was happening to us when we knew we weren't attracted to women. And neither of us wanted to stay there. We were women of God. Unfortunately, I had gone much further in my situation than she had in hers. But I was honest about everything. And I think for the first time, we both felt like, "Okay, so I'm not going crazy or being delusional. I'm not alone in this."

I think it was therapeutic for both of us to be able to talk to someone who knew exactly how we felt and what we were going through. And it was great that we had both confided in the same person as well. She and I would go on to develop a great friendship. She had become like a little sister to me and still is till this day.

Pastor Aye continued to counsel us both and check on our progress and was pleased to see that we hit it off so well and were a great help to each other. I was grateful to have someone I could talk to who understood my pain. But truthfully, my situation was a lot more complicated than hers because we had become involved physically, and as far as I knew, they had not. I encouraged her to not let it get to that place because it would be much harder to overcome.

Chapter 14
Broken and Contrite

I drove to North Carolina to my mother's house to pick up my daughter because her spring break was over. She loved going to spend time in North Carolina to be with her grandmother and see her cousins and her aunties. I moved to Atlanta before she was born and so she didn't get to grow up around our immediate family like the rest of her cousins did. And she, like the rest of her cousins, loved their grandma San (my mother). For Mani, she was much more fun to be around than I was because she always got away with more. And although it was good to have some time alone, had I known that I would get in trouble while she was gone, I probably would've opted to keep her home or go to North Carolina with her.

I got her off to school the next day, and when she got home after doing homework, she went to her usual, watching her favorite Neicy Wray DVD while I cooked dinner. This was routine for her almost every day. And almost every time she watched it, there was a certain part that brought great conviction on me and always had me choked up, heartbroken, and fighting back tears.

But today was different. Today, the conviction was a thousand times heavier, and it broke me all the way down. It wasn't unusual for me to be moved to shouting and crying by a song or a powerful Word, so my daughter understood that part, even at ten years of age. But this was heavy! I had no control! I cried and repented as I lay prostrate in my snot and tears unable to move until I was released.

As I lay there crying, broken, and hurting, I heard the Holy Spirit say as clear as day to me, "You have to tell one of them. Doesn't matter which one, but you have to call tonight and tell them what's going on." I knew He was speaking of Neicy Wray or Minister Claudia. And I had long known that I needed to speak to one of them about it, but I couldn't bring myself to do so. But there was no denying the voice of God speaking to my heart and the contrition heavy in my spirit. As hard as it would be to do it, I knew I had to. I needed more accountability and I just felt like these ladies would deal with me in a way that would put me in my place. And it wasn't going to be pretty.

I met Chloe at the conference that they brought me to and gave me a platform to minister to their girls. It's only right that I let them know that this was going on.

I absolutely hated that I had to. This was utterly embarrassing and degrading to have to admit to people that I admired so much, my incredible failure. Moreover, I couldn't even understand how I got here myself. Knowing that I had to confess this to them only added to my pain because I can feel their disappointment in me just thinking about it. How do you try to explain something like this and make them believe that this wasn't something you wanted because you never thought about women like that ever before? *You're going to sound like a fool*, I thought.

I had completely interrupted my daughter's time of watching and dancing to the DVD as she felt led to come over and console me in my despair. After a while, I was finally able to get up off the floor and go wash my face, which I seemed to be doing in vain since the tears continued to flow.

While I was getting myself together, Chloe called. Surely, she could tell immediately that I had been crying and she asked me what was wrong. I told her about watching the DVD and the conviction that came over me. She said to me, "I don't know why you keep watching the video when you know what it does to you." I had told her of other times when the strong convictions would come over me while watching the DVD and always at the same part of the DVD. But what was I supposed to do? Tell my daughter she couldn't watch the DVD because it convicts Mommy of her sins? Certainly not! And actually, I welcomed the conviction. I wanted out! And I believe this made me a little stronger every time.

As Chloe and I continued to talk, I told her that this time was different and that the Holy Spirit spoke to me and told me that I had to confess to either Neicy Wray or Minister Claudia, but I had to tell one of them *tonight*. As much as I admired Neicy Wray, I knew that I didn't want to talk to her about it. I'm not sure why. I just wasn't ready to have this conversation with her. So I knew it would have to be Minister Claudia.

Chloe didn't take it well that I was now telling someone else about this situation. Just as she did when I told her I was going to tell Pastor Aye, she began to beg me not to tell Minister Claudia. She expressed how she thought it could turn out really bad if I told them and to let them find out on their own if it was meant for them to find out. She thought I should just leave it alone. To me, her response was more confirmation that I should tell them. The Word of God tells us to confess our sins one to another (James 5:16), and if anyone deserved to know, they did!

At this point, I was willing to deal with however they responded. I just needed to be obedient to the Holy Spirit and confess. I thought of how horribly wrong this could go and how angry they could respond and how my reputation and career/ministry could be over. And still, it didn't matter. It was a chance I was willing to take. I had to confess.

Chloe would continue to plead with me not to say anything to anybody else about it and to just let it go. I couldn't agree to that. So when we hung up, we didn't do so on good terms.

After I got off the phone with Chloe, I called Minister Claudia, but I got her voice mail. I left a somber message for her to call me back as soon as she possibly could and that it was kind of important. I then sent her an e-mail and a text stating the same. I know she's a really busy woman, so I wouldn't be surprised if it took a while for her to respond. It didn't. She responded by text to let me know she would call in the next fifteen minutes. They were probably the longest fifteen minutes I've ever waited in my life. My heart was beating fast, and my soul was hurting from all that I had to confess to her, trying to brace myself for her response and how to respond to her response.

These were the longest and, at the same time, the shortest fifteen minutes I've ever waited.

She finally called and I answered, trying to sound like I was okay, but she already knew something was wrong. She said, "Hey, Chinnita." She always addressed me by my name, which wasn't unusual, but it was a bit comical because she seemed to pronounce every letter in my name, and she always had a joyful tone in her voice. It was really going to hurt to give her this disappointing news.

"How are you?" in her Nashville vernacular.

"Ummm, not doing so well, Minister Claudia," I responded. She asked me what was going on, and I was trying to muster up the courage to get it out. I paused for a while to try to keep from crying before I could tell her what I needed to tell her. Forcing myself to hold back the tears, I managed to tell her that I had messed up pretty bad. She asked me what happened. I began to tell her that I had become friends with several of the girls at the conference and that one in particular became attracted to me. At this point, I began to cry. I told her weeping that I had never been with or even thought about being with a woman before in my life but that now I had become attracted to her too and that we had slept together. I told her that she was seventeen years younger than me and that she came on to me and that I was unable to resist her. I apologized a hundred times, and by now, she probably had a hard time understanding what I was saying because I was crying so hard.

"Chinnita, sweetheart," she said, "I need you to calm down."

I was hurting so bad that I didn't have time to think about how she would respond to what I just told her, but I know I didn't expect her to respond the way that she did, especially not as a woman of God!

She asked me to calm down again so that I could hear what she had to say. I tried to gather myself so that I could stop crying, but the best I could do was bring it down to a whimper as the tears continued to stream down my face. No matter how bad she came at me, I needed to hear what she had to say to me. Whatever it was, I deserved it! This was awful, and I could've messed it up for everybody for giving in to my flesh and not counting up the cost. Whatever she would dish out, I was bracing myself to take it.

"Listen, my dear," she said. "You cannot walk in this condemnation. Sweetheart, you have to let this go. Did you repent?" she asked me.

"Yes, I did," I said, still whimpering.

"Well, honey, you don't repent and walk in condemnation. Now, I admit, it's pretty heavy and it's bad and I hear your hurt and your brokenness, but when you repent, you trust that you are forgiven and move forward and sin no more."

Then she asked me about "the girl" and how she was doing. I told her that she was fine and that she didn't want me to tell her about our situation. I told Minister Claudia that I had confided in my pastor in Knoxville long before anything happened. And she knew of my friendship with Allison because they went to the same church. I continued to tell her that Allison and I were no longer friends because of this situation and that she was the first person I told about it.

I told her about the DVD and how convicted I was every time my daughter watched it, but that tonight, the Holy Spirit arrested me and told me that I had to call one of them tonight, and I chose to call her. She told me she was glad I did so that she would know how to pray for me and because I didn't need to be walking in condemnation like I was. She told me she would talk to Neicy Wray and tell her what happened. I asked her please not to just yet. I just wasn't ready to deal with her knowing. I asked her to give me a minute with that. She told me she would and to let her know when I was ready so she could tell her. I told her I would. She began to pray for me, and when she was finished, she told me that I would be all right and that I would overcome this and that she would be checking on me. I told her I would appreciate that. I thanked her for praying for me, and again, she said, "You're gonna be fine, my dear." We hung up.

Now I was broken all the more! because I don't know what kind of response I expected, but I know that I didn't expect that. What is wrong with these people? Don't they realize what I've done is despicable and wretched? *How dare they respond to my sin with love and compassion! Where is the rebuke? Where is the lashing of how wretched I am for being so weak in my flesh, committing the abominable! A minister of the Gospel and a Christian comedian... If anyone should know better, you should!*

You don't deserve to stand onstage and minister through laughter. You're unworthy to be a minister of the Gospel until you get your flesh in order!

This was what I expected to hear. And for some reason, I thought that's what I needed to hear.

Why did I think like that? And was that how I was responding to others who had fallen short in their walk with Christ? Did I condemn others and deem them unworthy for their failures? I'm pretty sure I did, because I don't remember responding to anyone in their failures the way that Pastor Aye and Minister Claudia responded to me. Somehow, without downplaying my sin, they responded with love and compassion and taught me about GRACE! I thought I needed to be dragged through the mud and told how much of a disgrace I was to the Kingdom of God. Surely, in my mind, that's what I deserved.

Their response to my confession opened my eyes to what was wrong in my heart and maybe even to why I was here, why God allowed this to happen to me in the first place.

Now it was all beginning to come together and make sense. Unfortunately, I would go through this hell to see that I didn't get what I deserved for my failures. That, in the midst of it all, God's grace and mercy continued to keep me. Even though I fell a hundred times it seemed, His grace kept me. I never stopped trying, and He never gave up on me. I knew my heart for God was sincere, and I knew this wasn't me. But I was in a bad way. It felt like an addiction. I wanted out. I hated it, but my flesh longed for her. And I would give in to my flesh. Now, I could identify with some of my sisters who were addicted to crack cocaine and I couldn't understand why they just wouldn't fight to overcome it. I realized now that it's not that they didn't fight to overcome it. It was just that the fight was more than what I realized. It wasn't just a natural battle but a spiritual one as well. And they weren't saved and didn't know how to fight. For we wrestle not against flesh and blood, but against principalities and spiritual wickedness of this world (Ephesians 6:12). I now saw their struggle differently, and I now responded differently.

I can tell you that if this had happened to me while I was unsaved in the world, I probably would've been consumed by it and probably would've bought into the lie that I was gay and just didn't know it, and now it's manifesting itself. But because I know the Lord as my redeemer and savior, I knew how to fight against this evil spirit that had seduced me. I knew I wasn't gay. I knew this was the work of the devil. How does one go from never having an attraction to women to all of a sudden being attracted to one for no reason? The devil! And although I found myself doing some seriously ungodly things, I refused to buy the lie. I knew who I was and I knew whose I was.

I was and am a child of the Most High God! And I believed what His Word said about me. I believed that whom the Son set free was free indeed (John 8:36). I was already free. I just had to walk in it. It was hard, but I can do all things through Christ who strengthens me (Philippians 4:13). I was already victorious! I overcome by the blood of the Lamb and the Word of my testimony and love not my own life, even unto death (Revelations 12:11). The blood of Jesus gives me strength to overcome the powers of darkness, and the truth of my testimony or confession destroys the accusations of the enemy! God has given you power to tread upon the heads of serpents and scorpions, and over all the powers of the enemy: that nothing shall by any means hurt you (Luke 10:19 KJV). I had to trust the power given to me by God to crush the head of the enemy and walk in the righteousness of Christ that I am.

Now sometimes this is much easier said than done depending on your war clothes. It's good to stay suited and booted in the "full armor of God" (Ephesians 6:11–17) so that when the enemy targets you, you are able to stand. And continue to stand on the Word of God.

All of us who are determined to walk according to the will of God become a target for the enemy at some point in our lives. He's not so concerned with those who are neither hot nor cold. He wants the ones who are on fire for God. He wants the ones who are unashamed of the Gospel of Jesus Christ and are out to win more souls for Christ. The enemy doesn't go after Christians who aren't making any noise. He attacks the ones who stand and speak boldly for Christ. His desire is to shut them down.

If you look back on some of the saints of God who had horrible public failures, they were more than likely someone who stood boldly for righteousness. And in spite of their failures, they repented and were restored and resumed their ministries representing Christ now wiser, stronger and better than they did before. Because many are the afflictions of the righteous, but the Lord delivers him from them all (Psalm 34:19).

It's not a matter of "if" you will fall but "when." If the enemy doesn't come for you, you're probably not a threat to him. And I don't say that to brag about my righteousness because clearly, in my desire to live wholly holy, I failed miserably! But through my failure came great lessons, and I try to stay teachable. I knew there was a reason behind all of this. I was just trying to figure out what it was.

After telling Minister Claudia, she kept in touch with me to make sure I was okay and continued to minister to me when we talked. Although Chloe and I still talked, things were much different and I was breaking away. I would try to get her to talk to Minister Claudia or Pastor Aye, but she refused to. She wasn't happy about the fact that I talked to Minister Claudia because she could tell that the more I was being held accountable, the stronger I was, and soon, this would be over. I was grateful to God for Pastor Aye and Minister Claudia. God used them to get me through this with my faith intact. I had a heart to serve God faithfully, but I didn't deal with failure well. Mine or anybody else's. I wasn't the type to ridicule you and tell you how awful you were for falling, and as a matter of fact, I probably didn't say anything verbally most of the time. But the way I responded in my heart was all wrong. And because the response in my heart was wrong, the way I responded in my actions toward you after that was wrong. Either I condemned you in my heart and stayed away from you or I probably wrote you off as "unsaved." It was never a blatant or obvious disdain. I would just chalk it up as "not serious about serving God." I was that "judgmental, legalistic, self-righteous" Christian. And if I can be honest, especially when it came to homosexuality. And that happened after I got saved because I've always known people who were gay. And truthfully, I was really naive when it came to homosexuality, but as long as you didn't come on to me, we were cool. But when I got saved, it bothered me to see people just walk in sin and especially that sin for some reason. Maybe because it's more visible in the church.

I didn't realize my own sin for looking down on others because of their failures. Not knowing that not everyone who is sinning is enjoying it. Some people are overtaken in a fault and had no intentions of being in the sin they are in and are baffled as to how they got there. Not only that, they hate it! And there are some who are in sin because they want to be, and they justify where they are with their own excuses. The problem is that most of the time, we don't know which is which, so we have to be careful about judging people.

When I came to Christ, I gave Him all of me. If I was going to do it, it would be all or nothing. I love the Lord with every fiber of my being and I hate sinning against Him. I was zealous for God, but with little knowledge, and that can be dangerous. As it proved to be for me, because God had to allow me to go through what I experienced just to teach me about Grace. Had I not been so judgmental and self-righteous, I probably wouldn't have had to go through such an ordeal.

The sad thing is, I had no clue that I was judgmental, self-righteous, or legalistic. Chloe would tell me I was judgmental. But I thought she only felt like that because I refused to let her think that what we were doing was okay. I remember her asking me why it was wrong. I responded, "Because God says it's wrong! We don't get to pick and choose which sins we agree with him on because of the ones we like."

When you have a heart to live wholeheartedly to please God, unfortunately, it can be easy to fall in to one of these categories, if not all of them. More than likely, if you are guilty of one, you're probably guilty of them all.

Because of my ignorance on grace, it's easy to see how I became legalistic (Colossians 2:20–23). But the self-righteous thing, I completely didn't get. Me, self-righteous! No way! (Pun intended.)

Self-righteousness is very easy to go undetected by the perpetrator unless it is blatantly pointed out in most cases by someone else. While writing this book, God instructed me to re-read the book of Job and to get a better understanding. I did. When I got to the end and saw how Elihu really went off on the three men who were accusing Job of sin, and then he turned to Job and corrected him on his self-righteousness to let him know that no matter how wonderfully righteous he was, that he wasn't God and wasn't there when God created the heavens and the earth. I'd read the story of Job several times, but it wasn't until this time that I got an understanding that God allowed Job to go through what he went through to show him his sin.

I knew he had to have sinned because he finally repented when God spoke to him and pretty much cosigned what Elihu had said to Job. But I still didn't really understand what Job's sin was. He was pleading his case and was basically telling the truth about his righteousness. But the problem was, Job wore his righteousness like a badge of honor, and this made him self-righteous. Job's problem wasn't anything he had done, but it was what he had become because of his ability to keep the law to the letter, and that was "self-righteous" (the Trumpet).

We unknowingly walk around with this pride in our hearts that seldom do we sin. Or at least, my sin is not this thing or that thing. Job made the mistake of comparing himself to other men and he ended up getting the big head because of his righteousness. In the end, once Job got his mind off himself and on to others, God blessed him with twice as much as he had before. Sometimes God uses the strangest things to draw men, and we don't get to choose what He uses to speak to us.

I, like Job, really could not understand why and how this was happening to me. I had just come off a mountaintop experience. I had just done a national television taping and was licensed to preach in August, I was being booked consistently, and I had just ministered through comedy at the conference of Neicy Wray, who was someone

I really looked up to. God was blessing me. I was being blessed all the way up to the very end of 2005. But 2006 would prove to be the ultimate test of faith for me and would come crashing down on me like a load of dirt.

Chapter 15
My Darkest Hour

This would be the year that I was divorced and celibate for three years (trinity). This would be eight years of me being born again (new beginning). This year, I would turn forty (wilderness). All these numbers were quite significant for me this year, and it would definitely prove to be a wilderness time for me. I have been through some things in my life that shook me to my very core, and I didn't know how I was going to bounce back. But this year was my darkest hour yet.

But regardless of how bad things got, I never let go of God's hand. I stood strong in my faith and I continued to pray, praise, and worship God—even though many times I felt unworthy to. There were times the enemy tried to make me think I wasn't really saved, but I knew that was a lie. Through it all, I knew God was still with me. The conviction in my heart kept me aware of His presence. I don't know about you, but there were times when I've messed up and seemingly so bad that I think to myself, *God, I understand if I don't wake up in the morning.* And when I open my eyes and realize He blessed me in spite of me to see another glorious day, I'm eternally grateful and humbled, because I recognize God's grace and mercy over my life in spite of my failures. He is long suffering toward me. And that's not a license to keep falling short just because we know He is patient and full of loving kindness. But we should be moved to be stronger in our walk with Him. While in this situation with Chloe, every day was a brand-new mercy to get it right. Even after I had fallen again and again (Romans 2:4).

I wanted more than anything to live my life pleasing to God. I hated being here, but it had taught me a lot. I'd learned to stop being judgmental, legalistic, and self-righteous. I learned that not everybody who is in sin wants to be there. That some are fighting to get out just like I was so they can serve God with clean hands and a pure heart. Most of all, I learned that any of us can fall into any sin at any given time for any reason, and it may not even be something you enjoy doing.

During the summer of 2006, I was finally able to break free of Chloe much to her chagrin. Trust me, she gave me an earful before it was all over. But I was determined to get out. I was always reminded in my spirit that "the longer I stayed, the harder it would be to get out" (Selah). I knew I couldn't let this linger, and it had already gone on too long and should have never been entertained in the first place. Pastor Aye and Minister Claudia did a great job of checking in on me and holding me accountable, and I was mindful to always be honest with them, even when it wasn't pretty. I knew that if I was dishonest about anything, I would only be hurting myself and giving the enemy the upper hand in this situation. God knows I didn't want that, so I told the truth no matter how ugly or disappointing it was. I knew they were praying for me because I was growing stronger every day until I could just walk away, no matter how much she cried or cussed at me. Finally, it was over. Yes, she called again and again and again. But I would not answer her calls or her text messages. It hurt not to, but this had to stop.

A few weeks later, I received a letter and a CD in the mail with music from India Arie on it that I guess was supposed to describe her feelings of "love and forgiveness."

Again, even though I'd never heard them, the songs were quite appropriate. The letter and the music made me cry. I hurt for both of us, but I refused to call her. I never responded. Soon, she would no longer attempt to contact me, and life resumed as normal—somewhat. Thoughts of her flooded my mind, and there were many times I wanted to give in and call her. But I knew all too well how far back it would set me, and I wanted desperately for this to be over forever. Never to resurface again!

There was another conference that year, and Minister Claudia thought that I definitely should come. That even though I wasn't performing, I should be there because of all that I had gone through with that situation. To me, that was the reason I shouldn't be there. It was the last place I wanted to be truthfully, but she insisted that I come and bring my daughter. She would make sure that we had free tickets to everything. My daughter was excited and really wanted to go. So against everything I felt, she and I packed up and went to Nashville for the conference for three days. This one was much bigger but not necessarily better. Aside from my daughter enjoying herself, I really hated having to be there. I didn't really know any of the grown people there, and although many of the young girls knew me from the year before, I didn't know them. One in particular remembered me and my daughter from the year before, and she asked if she could take my daughter into the concert portion with her. Cute little kid wants to hang with my daughter, is what I was thinking. She and my daughter were about the same height, but she was actually twenty-three years of age. She looked like she was no more than fifteen. She promised she would take good care of her, and my daughter really wanted to go in. I really didn't want to, so I agreed and we exchanged cell numbers so she could reach me when they were done. I sat in the lobby and enjoyed the concert from afar. Didn't really care to be in there with a bunch of screaming teens and young ladies. I didn't get to talk to Minister Claudia much because she was so busy with the conference, but she made sure we were taken care of. My daughter was enjoying herself, but personally, I couldn't wait for it to be over. I hated being there because of what I had done. God knows I didn't want to run into Neicy Wray because I had allowed Minister Claudia to tell her weeks before I got there, and she too responded with love and compassion. Unbelievable! She told Minister Claudia that she wanted to talk to me whenever she had some time after the conference was over. I agreed, but I really wasn't ready to talk to her about it.

On the last day of the conference, the young lady who took my daughter in the concert with her wanted to take pictures with me and my daughter before we all left. Her name was Symone. She had taken to my daughter and kept her with her during the last few events. When it was time to go, she and a friend of hers asked if we all wanted to go and get something to eat together and so we did. Her friend's name was Adele. We all met up at the Outback Steakhouse to eat. Adele was a bit older. She was in her thirties, married, and had a child. This was a getaway for her, and she was a big fan of Neicy Wray, as was Symone and all the other young ladies who pressed their way to the conference. Neicy Wray wasn't just a great Christlike example to young people but to anyone who knew her and followed her ministry.

I thoroughly enjoyed my time and fellowship with Symone and Adele. Little did I know I had just made two friends who would go on to be beautiful blessings in my life. Even to this day.

We all kept in touch with each other. Symone and Adele had already established a friendship, so they were pretty close. It was the end of October and Neicy Wray was coming to the civic center in Atlanta. Symone and Adele were coming to see her. We had all made plans to hang out, but I had an event on that Friday and would be back on that Saturday for another event in Atlanta as well. Symone was coming in with her older sister, and they were going to stay at my house. Adele and her husband and son were staying at a hotel. We were looking forward to this weekend since we hadn't seen each other since August but had spent much time on the phone. We were excited.

But this would be a weekend I would never forget. Just when you thought things couldn't get any worse because you had already been through the worse, right?

When I got to the airport, my oldest sister called me to give me an update on my mother who had to go to the hospital the night before. She told me that they couldn't find anything wrong and kept sending her home even though she was in pain. This had happened twice already. Now be mindful, I live five hours away from my family who lives in North Carolina. I instructed my sister over the phone to take her back to the hospital and tell them not to release her until they figure out what was wrong with her. Meanwhile, my flight has been delayed three times, and it's looking like I'm not going to make it to Chicago for my event because it's getting late.

Eventually, the flight was cancelled, and all the other flights were overbooked. I called the agency to let them know that I won't make the show and they contacted the promoter. Symone and her sister were coming in that night so since I was already at the airport. I just stayed and picked them up. I had gotten an update on my mom that they found that she had a UTI and that was where some of the pain was coming from, but they continued to do more tests on her, and my sister would let me know as soon as she found out more information.

I picked up Symone and her sister, and we all went out to dinner. While we were at dinner, my sister called with an update. She asked me where I was and told me to go somewhere private. I got up from the table and walked outside the restaurant. My sister Beverly began to tell me that the doctors had found that my mother's heart wasn't leaking... it was pouring blood into her body. A valve in her heart had detached, and blood was pouring out into her system. There was nothing they could do because my mother had a weak heart and she wore a pacemaker. If they tried to operate, it was almost a guarantee she wouldn't make it. They couldn't do anything. They told her that my mother's organs were shutting down, and they didn't know how long it would take. It could take a few days or a few weeks and that all they could do was wait. I was devastated! Surely, I was not hearing what I thought I was hearing! I was crushed! I began to cry, and I asked my sister how my mother was doing, and she said they gave her some morphine for the pain and she was sleeping. We cried together over the phone, heartbroken. This cannot be happening.

She needed to call my other sisters to let them know what was going on. I cried and prayed after we hung up and tried to gather myself to go back in the restaurant to be with Symone and her sister. They asked me if everything was all right. I told them that my mother wasn't doing well. The mood was somber for the rest of the night. When I got home, my daughter was shocked to see me because I was supposed to be out of town. But she was ecstatic to see Symone. She had been looking forward to her coming all week. My sitter left to go home shortly after I got there.

I wanted to leave and get on the road to go be with my mother. My heart was hurting and I wanted to be with her. She was my best friend. I was crazy about her and she was crazy about me. We fought like cats and dogs, but we always made up quickly. We didn't always have a good relationship. We actually didn't have a relationship at all when I was younger. My mother was a heroin addict when we were growing up, and she put us through a lot. Especially me. For some reason, she hated me and was always really abusive to me. So I stayed as far away from her as I could because no matter what I did, I could never please her. She hated the sight of me. Out of six girls, I was the only one she treated with such disdain. She was pretty awful to my oldest sister Beverly too, but I always got the worst of it, physically and verbally. Bev left home at an early age.

But while I was in college, God began to change our relationship. By the time I graduated, my mother had kicked her heroin habit and was a completely different person. I think she had clarity now that she was sober and began to realize the damage she had done to all of us.

I think it blessed her to see that I had done something good with my life and that I didn't let my surroundings make me a statistic but that I overcame my circumstances in spite of, only by God's grace. I think that made her proud for once. And for all the names she had called me and all the times she told me I was nobody and wasn't going to be nothing, she was wrong. And as much as I tried to stay out of her path when I was younger, I now wanted to be around her and she liked being around me. We formed an unbreakable bond. Her life had changed completely since she was no longer doing drugs. She had remarried and they had bought a home together. She and my stepfather were great supporters of me when I moved to Atlanta and started doing comedy. When I was broke, they would make sure I had something to eat. They would drive down and visit me to make sure I was okay.

When things took off for me, I took good care of them. My stepfather died in 2001. We were all devastated because he had been more of a father to us than any of our fathers had been. My mother now had to learn how to take care of the bills and live alone, something she had never done. I was crazy about my mother, but although she had overcome her drug addiction, she still wasn't saved and still had a slight drinking problem. And she was diagnosed with congestive heart failure. The damage she had done to her body while abusing drugs would catch up with her in her late forties and early fifties.

When I got saved and committed my life to Christ and switched to Christian comedy, my mother was still my biggest supporter. She loved my walk with the Lord, but she just could not bring herself to make the commitment.

I prayed fervently for my mother's salvation, so much so that I would be in tears many nights laboring in prayer for her. Sometimes she would call me and ask me to pray for her or explain a scripture to her. She knew she needed to make the commitment, but she just wasn't ready.

My mother and I talked every day! God put an urgency in my spirit to minister to her one day in particular, and He must have prepared her heart because, to my surprise, she was ready to surrender. I led her in the prayer of salvation and she received Christ as Savior. This was two months before I got tonight's bad report.

As much as I wanted to go home, I couldn't because I had another show to do in Atlanta the next night. I wanted to cancel it and get on the road, but I knew I would leave them in a jam if I did. I had to wait it out. My heart was heavy, but I got through it. After the show, I went to the civic center to meet up with Symone and my daughter. They had ridden with Adele and her family to the concert and I was to pick them up. While there, I ran into Minister Claudia and we talked for a moment. She could tell my heart was heavy and she asked if I was okay. I told her what was going on with my mother and she talked to me for a bit and told me she would be praying for her.

I had to find my daughter and Symone and her sister to get them home. I wasn't in the mood to be in the midst of all this joy and laughter.

The next day, I was packed and ready to hit the road and waiting for my sitter to get there to keep my daughter because I wanted to stay and spend as much time with my mother as I could. Ironically, this was the day my sitter had lost her dad three years ago to a heart attack in his sleep. We were all pretty close. They were like family, so this day was already sentimental. Everyone met up at my house to say their goodbyes. Adele and her husband and son were taking Symone and her sister to the airport for me so that I could get on the road. Adele wanted to pray for me before we all left. I agreed but it was taking everything I had to hold it together. When we all got together and joined hands to pray, I broke down in tears because I couldn't believe my mother's life was in jeopardy.

It was best that it happened before I got on the road for the next five hours even though while driving, tears would stream down my face at times, wondering what my sisters and I were about to have to face.

I talked to my mother while on the road. She had a room full of visitors. And she was a little irritated and uncomfortable. She wanted to know how soon I would get there. I told her I was less than an hour away and I couldn't wait to see her. She told me she loved me so much and I told her the same and we hung up.

I arrived about thirty minutes later only to find out that my mother had passed five minutes before I got there. Everyone was standing around crying. I stood at the foot of her bed looking at her lifeless body in disbelief. I walked over and sat on the bed, leaned over to hug her, and kiss her face as many times as I could. She was gone, but she was with God. My heart was broken, but my spirit rejoiced and I was so proud of her. I couldn't thank God enough for answering my prayers for her, and He did it in a way that I would have His blessed assurance that she was with Him. I cried a river of tears that night.

Three of my sisters and I went back to my mom's house that night. My oldest sister and I slept in her bed. This was unreal. We were awakened early the next day by the phone's ringing from friends and family calling because they heard she was gone. It was all too sudden. We found out Friday about her heart valve, and by Sunday, she was gone. My mother was beloved by everybody, some whom she used to do drugs with (and they were inspired by her sobriety) and some she had met through us. Everybody loved my mom because she was very kindhearted and a great cook, but she was straightforward with correction and didn't mind setting you straight about something. She didn't always say things the way you wanted to hear them, but she always told you the truth.

My sitter had called once I got to the hospital to see how my mom was doing and I had to tell her she was gone. She felt so bad for me and my sisters. I told her not to tell my daughter because I would deal with it when I got home. Adele and Symone called as well only for me to have to tell them she was gone when I got there. Symone cried and was feeling horrible because she felt like I would've gotten there on time had they not been at my house. I really couldn't understand why God wouldn't let me be there when she passed as close as we were, but I trust His will. If I wasn't there, I wasn't supposed to be.

Chapter 16
The Devil Will Find a Way Back

All of us were slammed with calls from friends and family as well as my mother's phone ringing off the hook. I had sent a text to some of my closest friends who knew her well and they began to call. My friend Jennifer would call me, crying so hard I could barely understand what she was saying. I knew she hurt for me because she knew my mother and I were extremely close. They all called to console me and tell me they would be at the funeral. Pastor Aye called and ministered to me while I cried uncontrollably. With a bit of authority in his voice, he told me to pull it together because I had to be strong. He knew my mother had given her life to God, and he reminded me to take comfort in knowing that she was with God. I absolutely took comfort in knowing she was with God, but I was going to miss my beloved. Who was going to call me every day to check on me? Who was I going to have stupid arguments with? Who was going to be my biggest fan now? She was gone, and she was never coming back.

It was only midmorning, and we were all being flooded with phone calls from everyone. Then it happened... Chloe called. A part of me wondered if she would call. But how did she find out? Honestly, part of me wanted to hear from her. I was hurting, and I was alone. I was the only one of my sisters who didn't have a companion to console them except for my sister Tonya, who was in a strict rehab at that time. They would only escort her to the funeral and take her right back.

Ironically, my mother had begged the courts to put her in that rehab instead of giving her jail time, again.

I answered the call and it was good to hear her voice.

"Hey," she said real soft and slow.

I think we both knew this was going to be a hard conversation to have for a few different reasons. She asked me how was I doing. I told her I was trying to be strong. She expressed her deepest sympathies for my loss and I thanked her. She knew I was crazy about my mom. She knew when we argued and almost everything we talked about. But my mother didn't know about her. I confided almost everything in my mother. But there was no way I was going to tell her I had an affair with a woman. It would've broken her heart. This was one secret I would have to keep from her. I just couldn't do that to my mother. She admired my walk with God, and she was trying to find the courage to make the same commitment.

Besides, my oldest sister called herself openly gay about nine years prior to this happening to me even though she was married. My sister had never shown interest in women ever before in her life. My sister and her husband were both using crack cocaine heavy for years. Drug use makes people do strange things while drugging. I believe she got into some of those strange things and got turned out and decided she wanted to be with women. When she told my mother, she was livid. I was the first person she called, fussing and going off, telling me that my oldest sister was in her house trying to convince her that she was gay. My mother was so mad and ready to disown her oldest child because of this. All I could do was laugh at my mother's response and she wasn't happy that I wasn't mad with her. I told her, "Mom, you can't just disown your child because she's gay." That's ridiculous!

My mother then asked me, "Well, how would you feel if your child came home and told you she was gay?"

I responded, trying to be facetious, "I would say, sweetheart, you're only two years old. It's too early for you to be calling your sexuality. Give it at least ten more years!" That only made my mother madder. I laughed harder.

"This is not funny, Chinnita!" my mother yelled at me. "This is not the time for jokes!" (Fond memories of Momma.)

I laughed at my sister too because it was just absurd. She had just been turned out. And now she was trying to be "proud" of it by telling our mother.

Little did I know that just a few years later, I would be hijacked by that same perverted spirit. And proud was the last thing I was about it. Staying there was not an option.

And here I was on this call with Chloe after not having talked to her for a few months now. But, I was glad she called. Like always, she would comfort me when I was having a bad day. And this was unreal for me. I was hurting like never before, but I had to be strong for my sisters so we could do what we needed to get done.

I asked her how did she find out, and surprisingly, she told me that Liz told her. "How did she find out?" I asked. She told me through social media on MySpace, how Symone put up a post asking for prayers for me and my family in the loss of our mother.

She said, "I know how close you and your mother were, so I know that I might be overstepping my boundaries by calling, but it was a chance I had to take. I had to make sure you were okay."

I told her I probably wouldn't be okay for a while but that I would get through it. I began to cry, and she listened. I guess not knowing what to say, she just held the phone until I got my bearing.

She then told me she wished she could be here with me. I told her that wouldn't be good. She chuckled and I did too. We talked for just a few minutes longer, and before we hung up, she assured me that she would call back to check on me later. I told her I would appreciate that.

Later that day, I also received a call from Sheila. She and I still talked but not as often as before. So it was good to hear from her. However, I was shocked to hear from Allison who called to express her condolences as well although she didn't seem to know what to say and almost like it was painful to have to call me. I told her I appreciated her calling, and it was really good to hear from her. We tried to talk a little bit, but the conversation seemed strained so I thought it best to let her go. She told me she would be praying for me, and I thanked her. We hung up.

Praise God, my stepdad had taught my mother well about keeping her business intact and paying her life insurance. We purchased her plot next to his when we laid him to rest. Earlier that year, my mother was able to come and see me preach at a church in Goldsboro, North Carolina. She was so proud. And now I would have to preach her eulogy. I prayed that she would be just as proud. I was proud of her. To stand in that pulpit and see so many people who traveled from near and far to pay their last respects to my mother, a woman who, at one time, made me afraid to watch the news because I was afraid there would be news of her demise broadcast because that's the type of life she was living. God gave me incredible strength that day, and it took everything in me to say farewell, but I took solace in knowing that I would see her again in heaven.

Chloe called me every day that week to check on me, and some days she kept me on the phone too long. There were even days we argued. I let her know that we could not continue to talk. I expressed my gratitude for her being there for me through such a trying time and that I really appreciated her but that I couldn't stay. This was the last thing she wanted to hear. I had been trying to prepare her for my departure from our friendship once again. And I was trying to do it nicely, but that's too much like right for Chloe. To be civil in an unwanted departure is senseless to her.

Needless to say, two weeks after my mother's death, I had to tell her we couldn't talk anymore. Now this shouldn't have been a shock to her because I had been telling her I couldn't stay the whole time we talked. She knew I had no intentions of staying, but maybe, she thought she could change my mind. She was being incredibly selfish. Here I was still grieving over the loss of my mother, and she wanted to fight about me leaving.

This was unbelievable. And as much as she tried, I refused to allow her to take me out of character.

I remember driving and talking to her on the phone on my way to a meeting, which I made her aware of. She didn't care. I tried to explain why it didn't make sense for us to continue talking on the phone anymore. She commenced to cussing me out and calling me all kinds of ungodly names and even using the Lord's name in vain, which I abhor, and she knew it. She was trying hard to get a reaction from me, but I wouldn't oblige. I listened to her rants and her rage, and if only she knew that the way she was acting was only giving me more strength to walk away and stay away, she would've stopped.

She was in a fit of rage, but it wasn't making me mad. It just made me realize all the more how I needed to run from her. And so I did. She continued to cuss and yell at me, and I just listened until she got so mad that she just hung up. I wanted her to be the one who hung up, so that if she called back, I wouldn't feel guilty about not picking up. And I didn't. Finally, it was over.

Chapter 17
Out of Egypt

I wouldn't talk to Chloe again for almost two years. And when I did, I called her. My conscience got the best of me, and as much as I was glad it was over, I didn't want her to hate me. One day, I was compelled to call her and apologize. I called, and there was no answer. I wasn't sure if she saw my number and just decided not to answer or if she just wasn't available. I was really nervous anyway so I just hung up. Later that day, it was heavy in my spirit to call her again, and so I did. Again, it went straight to her voice mail. This time, I left a message explaining why I called, that I didn't want anything but to apologize and that I hope she didn't hate me and could forgive me for everything. Then I hung up.

Even though I wasn't able to speak to her over the phone, because I was able to leave a message I felt relief. I no longer felt a need to contact her.

A few days later, I got a call from her. I answered but she hung up. I didn't try to call her back. Later that evening, she called again. I answered and said hello, but she held the phone for a moment before responding. I waited until she finally spoke and asked me how was I doing. I was amazed at how her voice had matured in just two years.

We talked for a long time catching up on each other's lives that day and would go on to continue talking as if though it was just yesterday that we last talked. Of course we expressed our hurt and sadness to all that had transpired. She had actually started seeing some other girl that lived in Jacksonville as well. As disappointed as I was that she was still in that lifestyle, it didn't bother me that she was seeing someone else because I loved our friendship, but I didn't want her to want me and I didn't want to want her. But in the midst of all the foolishness, we had a really cool friendship. That's what I missed about her. That's all I wanted from her. And even if I had to live without that, I would be fine. Unfortunately, I was still single and waiting on my man of God. And there were prospects, but they weren't approved by God. I had been through too much to settle for less than God's best for me.

We had gotten to a place where she would tell me about her girlfriend and what they did that day. I'm not sure if she was telling me to make me jealous, but it wasn't working. Her having somebody else meant I didn't have to worry about her trying to get with me, so I really didn't care. By the way, Pastor Aye and Minister Claudia were both informed that we were communicating again. They both admonished me to be careful and would ask about us talking periodically.

Chloe and I had started talking a lot on the phone again, and even though she had someone, she had started flirting with me again, and I would mostly just brush it off, mostly. I fought it off because I just didn't want that. We had come too far and were doing good as friends. I didn't want to go back there.

Minister Claudia had always warned me about protecting my daughter from the seducing spirits that comes from entertaining the spirit of perversion. I didn't think much of it since we were just friends now. Until one day, I was on my computer and all this porn stuff started popping up, and I went into my history and found that someone had been watching porn on my computer. I immediately thought it was my goddaughter who spends a lot of time with us and sometimes keeps my daughter when I'm out of town. I was livid! I couldn't believe she would be at my house watching porn. Are you serious! My daughter was at school and my goddaughter was at work but had planned on coming over later when she got off. Neither of them knew of my discovery yet, so I would ask them both when they were together so no one could lie. I went into my closet to pray. I was really upset and crying. I was almost certain it was my goddaughter until the Holy Spirit spoke to me and told me that it was my daughter. Now I was in agony! Not my daughter! This cannot be happening!

Later that evening, when we were all together, I asked them both at the same time. They both denied it completely. God had already revealed to me who it was, so I asked my goddaughter to go into the other room while I talked to my daughter. She was adamantly denying it but, after much interrogation, decided to come clean. My heart broke for her and all I wanted to do was get her some help. I made her apologize to my goddaughter for putting her through this when she could've just admitted the truth. And she apologized. The next day, I set up counseling for my daughter at our church, and she would have several visits for the next couple of months to help her overcome this.

In the meantime, Chloe and I were on shaky ground with our friendship because she was flirting a lot more now and we were beginning to argue again. She was still with her girlfriend, and still to me, this was probably the only reason we could maintain a friendship and be civil. Sometimes it seemed as if she tried to make me jealous as often as she could by telling me about her day with her girlfriend. She even seemed to get frustrated that I never reacted to it the way that she wanted me to. One day she went off on me and asked me why wasn't I fighting for her.

"Why don't you care that I'm with her when you know I'd rather be with you? Why aren't you fighting for me?"

I yelled back at her, "Because, Chloe, I am fighting for me! That's not what I want!" We were both near tears. She wanted answers that I wasn't sure she was ready to hear. And honestly, I cared so much for Chloe that I knew not having her in my life was going to hurt. It was complicated and hard to explain. But I realized that I had come back into her life only to have to walk out again. It wasn't fair and it wasn't right, but there was no way I could go back to Egypt. Especially since another one of my goddaughters found porn on my computer again after I thought my daughter had gotten past it. Minister Claudia and Pastor Aye had warned me about those perverted spirits infiltrating my home, and now it had manifested itself in the form of porn addiction through my twelve-year-old daughter. Again, I was heartbroken to see my daughter going through this and all because of me. I talked to Pastor Aye, and he told me in a higher-pitched voice than he normally speaks, "As long as you are talking to that girl and entertaining those spirits, they will infiltrate your home and wreak havoc!" I knew what I had to do. This was where I draw the line.

When Chloe called me that day, I told her what was going on, and that again, I had to go. That this would be the last time we would talk. In typical hotheaded Chloe fashion, she commenced to cussing me for everything she could think of. I tried to calm her down to talk to her rationally since this would be our last conversation. I wanted us to leave each other amicably this time. But she had no desire to be rational or amicable. And either she didn't believe this would be our last time or she was just too mad to care. I understood her hurt and her anger and the last thing I wanted to do was cause her anymore pain. That was not my intention at all. And if she knew anything about me, she should've known that was never my heart toward her. But nothing was worth putting my daughter in harm's way. She didn't care. All that mattered to her was again, I had disappointed her. She told me how much she hated me and promised me that this was the last time I would ever do this to her again, and she hung up on me.

The irony is that it was the exact day a year before that we had reconnected. The same day we connected, to the very day a year later, we disconnected. This time forever.

I never called her again, and she never called me. It was hard, but there was no way in Hades that I was going to allow the enemy access to my child through spirits of perversion! I don't think I understood at first the danger I was putting my daughter in with spirits of perversion lurking. But after we stopped communicating, my daughter never had any more problems with porn again. Coincidence? I think not!

Chapter 18
A Thorn in My Flesh

Years would pass by and Chloe was long gone from my life. Unfortunately, thoughts of her were not, nor was the guilt and shame of my failure. I pressed every day to put it all behind me but the enemy refused to let me forget. I still cried a lot most of the time in disbelief that I fell into such sin. Still trying to wrap my head around all that had happened. Still learning to live without my mother and still grateful she never knew and somehow feeling partly responsible for God taking her as punishment for my sin. Still celibate and desiring my man of God in the worst way. But God knows I've been through too much to settle. I have no desire to go through the rest of my life alone, but at the same time, I'd rather be alone than in a miserable relationship. Been there, done that.

I'm in a hard place in life. I am twice divorced, the single mother of a teenage girl who battles sickle cell anemia and is in and out of the hospital now more than she has ever been. Her father has never been in her life and has done nothing for her. I struggle financially because work can be inconsistent in entertainment. I'm praying, preparing, and waiting for my man of God, but my Father has yet to oblige me. This I cannot understand for the life of me. I have been single and waiting for my man of God since I was thirty-seven years old and now I'm in my late forties and my daughter is about to leave for college. Not only am I still single, but when she leaves, I will be all alone. And to add insult to injury, all of my friends are married. But hey! I won't complain! It could be worse.

When my daughter left for college, it was harder than I thought it would be for me. I had bragged about how I was going live my life to the fullest because I had spent the last eighteen years making sure she was fine. When she was gone, the house was cold and empty. I would sleep in her bedroom most nights. I had freedom, but nothing to do with it. I did enjoy not having to rush back home from gigs but being able to take my time and maybe stay an extra day or so. She was enjoying college and I was enjoying what I could of my grown and free life with nothing to do. Unfortunately, idle time is the devil's workshop as they say.

It was 2015, and before I knew it, I found myself having to fight my way out of this situation again. This time it wasn't Chloe and this time it was my fault. Here it was nine years later, and I had fallen back into something that I hated. It happened all of a sudden; nothing was planned, and nothing led up to it. This was not what I wanted, and praise God, neither did she, so this time I wasn't fighting alone.

Again, I didn't waste any time letting Minister Claudia know. When I called her, I was broken and I had no explanation. Again, she was compassionate, and even though I could tell she was disappointed, she stuck with me and helped me through it once again. I didn't tell Pastor Aye yet because I was just too embarrassed and disappointed in myself. When I finally did tell him, he did kind of fuss at me and I think it was easier for him to this time because I wasn't crying. He had a long talk with me and helped me realize that the enemy played on my loneliness and she was convenient. Odd that he would say that, because I would actually tell her that. But this time, I kind of knew what to expect and how to fight.

Now please understand something, we didn't stop because we got exposed or caught. We stopped because it wasn't what either of us wanted. Neither of us was gay. We were both celibate and waiting for our men of God when this happened. And more than anything, we stopped because of our love for our Savior and Lord. We want to live according to His will. And there is no confusion in the Word of God as to how sinful this is. Roman 1:18–32: "If you're confused, it's because you want to be to justify your sins."

So please understand, I'm not telling you my business because I have to. I'm putting this out there first to those of you who are oblivious that this is going on in the church to be aware of what's happening in your pews. Being with a woman was the last thing I'd ever wanted or even though about. So if it happened to me... how many other people were going through this and not saying anything because they were either embarrassed and ashamed or consumed by it and believing that they were gay and just didn't know it. Homosexuality in the church is not breaking news. But rarely do you hear about women dealing with it.

When this happened to me the first time, I couldn't believe it was happening. It didn't make sense. I knew it was spiritual warfare. I didn't understand it, but I knew this was the work of the enemy. I'm not going to indulge in something I have no interest in just because I can. I knew this wasn't me. And I knew I had to overcome it so that I could expose the enemy and his tactics. Many of us are vulnerable to the enemy because we are ignorant to his schemes and tactics.

I was ignorant of his tactics and never imagined him coming at me like that. I was blindsided! That was the last thing I ever thought I'd be doing. And as embarrassed as I was, I knew I had to find a way to speak up and tell my story so that anyone else who might be experiencing this would know that it is not an isolated incident. And that this was happening more than we care to talk about. And people are hurting in silence in the church. But I was raising my daughter as a single parent with a child who had a chronic illness, and I had no time to write a book nor did I really know how to. I vowed to jump on it once my daughter was in college. But then it happened again.

Now I felt unworthy to write the book. And I probably am, which is why I probably needed to write it. I knew I couldn't let another year go by without writing this book and putting the enemy on blast and letting people who are in bondage to anything, whether it be sexual immorality, drugs, alcohol, pornography, or anything they are ashamed of know that they are not alone. I believe this has been plaguing the church long before I spoke out but people are either scared of being shunned and ridiculed or crucified by the church. I can't worry myself about the church's response. That's in God's hands. I had to consider all that could happen to me for exposing my failures being a Christian entertainer and minister. But more than anything, I had to consider what could happen to all the souls who are secretly and silently experiencing this horror, feeling alone, unworthy and helpless. And all of a sudden, my reputation didn't mean so much anymore.

I pray that this book helps them find the courage to get the help that they need.

Let me make you very aware of the river of tears I've cried while writing this book. Having to relive this whole ordeal all over again, experiencing all the brokenness and confusion, the guilt and the shame, and even the hurt I knew Chloe had to feel. Losing my mother that same year just when I thought things couldn't get any worse.

But I was determined, and I pressed my way through it because I couldn't bear the thought of someone going through this not having anyone they could confide in or even having the courage to do so or just not even knowing what just happened to them, why, all of a sudden, they are in bondage to something they never desired.

I praise God for Pastor Aye and Minister Claudia. I don't know what I would've done without them. And I am eternally grateful for the time they sacrificed and the love and compassion they showed me while I was going through this. Through them, I saw Jesus and I learned how I was to treat people who fall short and especially when the fall is great. It was a hard lesson and one I wish I could've learned a different way but nonetheless, I get it now. Our job is to love them, and let the Holy Spirit do the rest.

Not that I learn to ignore people's sin but to be led by the Holy Spirit as to how to approach it (or not). And more than anything, to approach it with *grace*. I once heard someone say, "Preach the Word at all times, and when necessary, use words." How incredibly profound that was to me. It summed it all up. We can talk all day, but our actions are what have the greatest impact. And the greatest action is love (1 Corinthians 13).

When I found myself back in this situation for the second time, I was incredibly stumped. I remember feeling pretty much the same way when I was going through my second divorce. I never considered that I would be divorced once, because marriage was sacred to me and divorce wasn't an option (or so I thought). But everything was predicated on a lie and there was no way I could stay. I didn't remarry for seven years. And a year and a half after that, I would experience my second divorce. I was devastated. This could not be happening. I thought I took every precaution to make sure it didn't, except I married someone who didn't have the same mind-set. I was utterly embarrassed and ashamed and didn't want people to know that I had failed at marriage twice. This was something I refused to disclose to people if I didn't have to. Until God began to use me to minister to people who were either in a relationship about to get married or were already in a marriage and ready to give up. I hated divorce and I hated to see people give up on marriage so easy. And I had been in two of the worst situations you could think of. God would compel me to share my experiences with them to show them that what they were dealing with was spilled milk and it wasn't worth walking away from your marriage over. Then there were times I had to minister to couples to tell them they shouldn't get married or that they should wait. I vowed that I would never sit back and not say anything when I know I see something they don't see. Because when I married my first husband, we had mutual friends who knew of all of his indiscretions and things that they knew I didn't know and they didn't tell me anything! And all four of us hung out often. Who does that?

We got married at a chapel and these same people prepared dinner for us that day.

Had they told me about him before I married him, they could've saved me a lot of heartache and pain. So God took what was utterly embarrassing to me and used it to keep someone else from making the same mistakes. It was funny because I knew it could only be God bringing these people to me with these situations, asking a single, divorced twice woman for advice.

So having been free from that situation for nine years only to fall again in the same foolishness. What the...! That's all I could think. But as time progressed, I realized I had to be mindful not to let my guard down, and to walk circumspectly at all times.

There is nothing I love more than God my Father, and my heart's greatest desire is to live a life pleasing to Him. So to fall a second time really broke me down.

This second failure was a constant reminder that I was not above falling again. *It became a thorn in my flesh to keep me humble and rid me of self-righteousness* (2 Corinthians 12:7–9). I had to realize His strength is perfect in my weakness and to stop trying to do things in my own strength and to know that His grace was sufficient. Reminding me daily that I needed God's grace and mercy. Not only that, but that same grace needed to exude from me when others needed it. People need to see the same Amazing Grace Jesus shows me in my failures, shown to them when they fall. It's ridiculous to sing so wonderfully about God's amazing grace saving wretches like us, but when we see others' wretchedness, we don't see fit to extend that same Grace to them. It was a hard and costly lesson, but I finally got it.

There is no room for self-righteousness. And if we were busy dealing with the plank in our own eyes, we wouldn't be so quick to persecute people for the mote in their eye (Matthew 7:1–5). (And if you read that with an attitude of "I don't have a plank in my eye," then you are probably self-righteous.)

We need to cast down our legalistic ways. Just because people don't do things the way your church does, it doesn't make it wrong unless it completely goes against the Word of God. Stop making up your own rules and putting yokes on people thinking that's what piety is. Be careful not to walk in a Pharisee spirit thinking they were so holy and only causing people to stumble (Matthew 23).

By no means am I suggesting that you ignore sin in the body of Christ. We are called to holiness without which no man shall see God (Hebrew 12:14). We don't just keep sinning because we are covered by God's grace. "What shall we say, then? Shall we go on sinning so that grace may increase? By no means! We died to sin; how can we live in it any longer?" (Romans 6:1–2 NIV). "No one who lives in Him keeps on sinning. No one who continues to sin has either seen Him or know Him" (1 John 3:6 NIV).

We as people of God must do our part to hold each other accountable according to the Word of God (not our flesh). And understand that when you identify as a Christian, you put yourself in a position to be held accountable by other Christians. "But now I am writing you that you must not associate with anyone who calls himself a brother [or sister] but is sexually immoral or greedy, an idolater or a slanderer, a drunkard or a swindler. With such a man do not even eat" (1 Corinthians 5:11–13 NIV).

It sounds harsh but there is a method to the madness. This is God's way to show that blatant sin will not and should not be tolerated in the body of Christ, in hopes that the sinner will repent and be restored back to the body. When professing Christians refuse to come away from sin, God has given the church this charge. "Hand this man over to Satan, so that the sinful nature may be destroyed and his spirit saved on the day of the Lord" (1 Corinthians 5:5 NIV). "Do you not know that the wicked will not inherit the Kingdom of God? Do not be deceived: Neither the sexually immoral nor idolaters nor adulterers, nor male prostitutes, nor homosexual offenders nor thieves nor the greedy nor drunkards nor slanderers nor swindlers will inherit the Kingdom of God. And that is what some of you were. But you were washed, you were sanctified, you were justified in the name of the Lord Jesus Christ and by the Spirit of our God" (1 Corinthians 6:9–11 NIV).

God has given us His Word as instructions on how to deal with sin in the body of Christ. "Brothers, if someone is caught in a sin, you who are spiritual should restore him gently. But watch yourself, or you also may be tempted" (Galatians 6:1). And how we who find ourselves in sin are to respond.

"If you reject discipline, you only harm yourself, but if you listen to correction, you grow in understanding" (Proverbs 15:32 NLT).

"But He gives us even more grace to stand against such evil desires. As the Scriptures say, God opposes the proud but gives grace to the humble" (James 4:6 NLT). So we must humbly accept correction given according to the will of God.

Writing this book was both heartbreaking and therapeutic for me. There was no doubt in my mind that I had to write it because of the burden I felt for the souls (people) who are already experiencing or someday would be going through the same situation. Whether it be spiritual seduction or just blatant sin. Bondage of any kind is torture when your heart's desire is to live Holy for God.

I also had to write it because, for years, I have felt muzzled and unable to speak about this abomination publicly like I wanted to because I had not told my story in a proper way. I couldn't just put it out all willy-nilly and allow social media to run with it in every direction possible. Although I'm pretty sure the persecution will come. (Father, strengthen my heart.) I needed to convey my truth without interruption before the persecutors came hurling at me with their firey darts, challenging the truth of my experience. To just put it out there on social media would have been irresponsible and causing confusion and gossip. I needed it to be written so that when the questions come, you can refer back to "the book, for now it is written."

I watched so much take place regarding this sin of homosexuality unfold in America and the Gospel industry, wanting desperately to say what I knew about this spirit (because I had firsthand experience with it) and to call it out for the evil I knew it to be, but I couldn't. Because I had not shared my story. That didn't keep me from speaking against it... but I was only able to say "what thus sayeth the Lord" concerning it.

When I began writing this book, the more I wrote, the more I realized that as much as I was laying down my life to help someone else by writing it, I was being liberated too.

A great freedom came from telling my truth and taking off the mask. For years, I have felt caged and unable to truly fly and speak freely and openly because my failures made me feel unworthy to. And not just about homosexuality, but many things. That's what self-righteousness does to you. You think as long as you have no spots you are worthy and can say what you want to say, but when you fall and get dirty, even after you've repented you still feel unworthy. But when you fight to get out and overcome, God still sees you as the righteousness of Christ. "Although a righteous person may fall seven times, he gets up again, but the wicked will be brought down by calamity" (Proverbs 24:16, NET). Don't get complacent and began to justify your sins. No matter how much you may enjoy it.

I praise God for covering me all these years and not allowing it to be broadcast before I was ready to reveal it. Although I had purposed in my heart that if it should be revealed publicly, I would not deny it. It would've been hard to do but I knew that lying about it would only have me sinking deeper in sin.

I'm also grateful to Liz (Elizabeth) for not putting me on blast when she could have. I know it was a lot to keep and probably burdensome, especially since she didn't like me anyway. And she was young, and normally, young people aren't mature enough to keep something like that about a well-known person secret. And even though she didn't care for me, she did. Thank you, Liz. I appreciate you for that.

However, little did Liz know that she played a big part in my overcoming and getting free, because I knew she was utterly disappointed in me and I let her down. She had seen me on TV and had become somewhat inspired by my testimony switching from secular to Christian comedy, only to come to know me vicariously through Chloe, and this is the behavior she would witness from me. Ugh!

I know the feeling all too well. There were many artists I admired from afar for the songs they wrote or sang or things they'd done that blessed me in some way, only to meet them and realize they didn't necessarily live the lives they sang or talked about. I never wanted to be that person. I want to practice what I preach and always walk and talk in a way that brings God glory. But I failed miserably in this case.

So even though she had great disdain for me because of my situation with Chloe, I cared deeply for her heart and what she thought about me. Therefore, it helped me fight with everything in me to overcome, for all the Elizabeths that know me now, and those that would eventually come to know me one way or another in the future, I pray that you always find me walking in integrity.

Chapter 19
Overcoming Strongholds and Spiritual Seduction

Part One

How to recover from failure or bondage

Spiritual failure can discourage the strongest of us in the body of Christ, especially if you are in a leadership position or have a public platform. And we have to be careful not to walk in condemnation when we fall. "There is therefore now no condemnation to them which are in Christ Jesus, who walk not after the flesh but after the Spirit" (Romans 8:1 KJV).

We have to realize that we are not the only one who's had tremendous failures. From the most spiritually mature to babes in Christ.

Let's look at 2 Samuel 11 and 12. (Read both chapters.) This is the story of King David's fall with Bathsheba and his efforts to cover up his sin even to a point of having an innocent man killed. People will go to great lengths to hide their sins. I have heard many people confess how they will go to their graves with their sins. I can only imagine the misery they are in trying to make sure it never comes to light, when clearly God is in control of that. Not only that, but you put yourself in danger of falling deeper into it and possibly never recovering. As well as passing it on to others in your bloodline.

In the story of David, we know that he thought he had gotten away with his sins until Nathan the prophet confronted him. When he was confronted, he repented and was quite penitent for his failures.

And this is where we get Psalm 51 written by David, expressing his sorrow and repentance for his sins with Bathsheba.

Steps to take to help you get free from sin and bondage

1. **Confess** – 1 John 1:9: "If we confess our faults, He is faithful and just to forgive us of our sins and cleanse us from all unrighteousness." When you confess, you agree with God that you have sinned. Take full responsibility for your sins. Don't make excuses for why you did it or try to place the blame elsewhere. I did it, I admit it, and I quit it! Yes, there are situations when we are overtaken and/or things happened before we knew what happened. There are even times when we sin unknowingly, but when you realize it, confess it and repent. Nathan had to confront David before he confessed. I suggest you confess before being confronted so as to deal with your sin before it spirals out of control. In these days and times, I doubt very seriously that a prophet will tell you of your sins. But try to make sure you are confiding in someone who is mature and takes no delight in gossiping about your failures. Confession is vital to you overcoming. You have to be honest with yourself before you can be honest with others. Unconfessed sin also hinders your prayers. Psalm 66:18: "If I had harbored sin in my heart, the sovereign Master would not have listened." And we cannot overcome what we will not confess or acknowledge. "They overcame him [the enemy] by the blood of the Lamb and by the Word of their testimony; and they loved not their own lives, even unto death" (Revelation 12:11). You have to confess your faults.

2. **Accept forgiveness from God** – I know this sounds like a "no-brainer," but even I had a problem with this one. I even had a hard time forgiving myself. After all these years, I thought that I had finally gotten over it and honestly forgiven myself, only to realize that I had not. I wept bitterly while writing and in my prayer time when reflecting back

on my failures. I realized that I hadn't really forgiven myself nor had I allowed the forgiveness God had provided me to manifest in my heart to give me peace to move forward.

To me, my sin was incomprehensible, therefore, too hard to believe that I repent, and just like that, it was gone into the sea of forgetfulness. The Word of God says. "As far as the east is from the west, so far has He removed our transgressions from us" (Psalm 103:12). You just got to believe it's done. This is why Jesus went to the Cross for us. "He was wounded for our transgressions, bruised for our iniquities, the chastisement of our peace was upon Him, and with His stripes, we are healed" (Isaiah 53:5 KJV). Now "Go and sin no more" (John 8:11 NLT).

2.5 **Forgive yourself** – I know it's hard to believe you've done something incredibly reprehensible and you're unable to comprehend what or why you did it. But if you have repented, you are forgiven. Jesus died for those very reasons nailing our sins to the cross so we wouldn't have to be condemned. Sometimes forgiving yourself is actually the hardest part of this process. But it has to be done. To not forgive yourself is an act of self-righteousness. Saying "There's no way I'm capable of stooping so low. Maybe others, but certainly not me." I don't deserve forgiveness if I failed so miserably. If Jesus can forgive you, are you better than Him? Put off self-righteousness! It is sin itself!

3. **Accept the consequences of your sins** – Hebrews 12:6–8 says whom God loves He chastens (disciplines or punishes). And if there is no chastening or conviction for your sins, you're more than likely not His child. There are always consequences for our sins and God is sovereign, He can do what He wants to. The problem is, we don't know how His hand will come down on us. So we pray for His mercy.

Nathan told David that the child he had with Bathsheba was going to die as a result of his sins. So David cried out to God to spare his child. He fasted and he prayed earnestly that God would relent and let the child live. But the child died seven days later. Nathan told David all that would befall his household because of his sin. And though David would live to witness much of it come to pass, he continued to serve the Lord with his whole heart. Only God knows the punishment that best suits us for our iniquities. But His judgment is always righteous and His justice is always true.

You may lose some things as a consequence of your sins: marriage, house, job, friends, family, trust. But keep going and keep serving God. His plans for your life were not thrown away because of your failure. As a matter of fact, God is more than able to turn it around for your good if you let Him. Joseph's brothers threw him in a pit and later regretted what they had done but could not reverse it because he was sold into Egyptian slavery. For years, they lived with the regret of what they had done to their brother and to their father for it broke his heart to think that his son was dead. But what the enemy meant for Joseph's harm worked out not only for His good but for his family and future lineage as well (Genesis 50:19–20 NIV). "All things work together for the good of them that love the Lord" (Romans 8:28).

4. **Sincere repentance** – Acts 3:19: Repent then and turn to God, so that He will forgive your sins. Acknowledge your sins and your weaknesses to God. Remember, be completely honest. He already knows your truth. Verbalizing your truth can be painful, but it can also be quite cathartic for you. God knows your sincerity or lack thereof. You won't fool Him, so don't even try to. The second letter of Paul to the Corinthians 7:10: "For Godly sorrow produces repentance leading to salvation, not to be regretted."

   David asked the Lord in Psalm 51:10–13 (KJV) to "create in me a clean heart O God and renew a right spirit within me. Cast me not away from thy presence; and take not thine Holy Spirit away from me. Restore unto me the joy of thy salvation; and uphold me with thy free spirit. Then will I teach transgressors your ways; and sinners shall be converted unto thee." True repentance is what God desires. You can't offer Him greater works or sacrifices. Psalm 51:16–17 says, "You do not desire a sacrifice, or I would offer one. You do not want burnt offerings. The sacrifices you desire is a broken spirit; a broken and contrite heart you, God Thou will not despise."

When you are truly repentant, you are remorseful for your folly. When we understand that sin separates us from God, we would be careful to live so that we could stay close to Him. People pay ridiculous premiums on insurance based on the what-ifs. What if I have an accident today or what if today is my last day? I need to be covered so my family won't experience financial hardships trying to recover if I don't have insurance to take care of me. If we could get that understanding with our walk with Christ, people wouldn't trifle with Christianity. Dwell in the shelter of the Most High. Don't allow sin to separate you from Him. The safest place to be is in His will.

5. **Humble yourself** – James 4:6–7: But He gives us more grace. That is why the Scriptures say, "God opposes the proud but gives grace to the humble." Submit yourselves then to God, resist the devil and he will flee from you.

You will not get free from sin without humbling yourself! There is no way around it. "Pride goes before destruction, and a haughty spirit before a fall" (Prov. 16:18). All those people with the unconfessed sin, talking about they will take it to their graves are walking in *pride*. This keeps them from sharing their failures because of the embarrassment they may face. But it will only keep them bound.

God calls us to humility. A sincere humility. If you have to tell people you're humble, that's a false humility. True humility is not spoken. It is illustrated.

When Nathan confronted King David, he didn't try to have the prophet killed or thrown in jail and he had the authority to do so. No, he humbled himself and admitted to the sins he was charged with and he sincerely repented in humility and accepted the consequences of his actions.

"For every one that exalteth himself shall be abased; and he that humbles himself shall be exalted" (Luke 18:14b KJV). After such an incredible failure, David was still described as "a man after God's own heart" (Acts 13:22 KJV).

6. **Seek accountability** – Understand this, YOU CANNOT DO THIS ALONE!!! You will have to have someone who will hold you accountable. If you don't know anyone, you can go to immediately that you can trust, then pray, and ask God to send you someone.

    Seek godly counsel so that they will help you according to the will of God. It should be someone grounded and rooted in Christ, someone spiritually mature who can handle your truth and love you through it.

    I was led by the Holy Spirit to go to both Pastor Aye and Minister Claudia. I went to Allison because she was my friend and that was more a decision made in my flesh that I didn't pray about before confiding in her and that didn't turn out so well. So make sure it's someone you know you can trust if it's not someone you were led to by the Holy Spirit.

    Submit yourself under their authority to hold you accountable and tell you the ugly truth in love.

    The enemy is hoping you will be too ashamed to ask for accountability and too proud to walk in it.

7. **Walk in integrity** – Be completely honest with yourself and whomever you confide in. Remember the enemy is counting on you to lie. He is the father of lies and he knows this will keep you in bondage to him. It was hard enough for me to admit to being with another woman. And the last thing I wanted to do was admit that I liked it. But to pretend that it disgusted me to no end would've been a lie. That's what I wanted to be able to tell them because that's what I always thought it was. But I did like it and they needed to know my true experience, without details, of course. I knew the only way to truly get free from this was to be truly honest.

Anything that you have to hide, you probably shouldn't be doing.

Psalm 51:6: "You desire truth from the inward parts."

8. **Stay in your Word.** David said, "Thy Word have I hid in my heart that I may not sin against you" (Psalm 119:11 KJV). "Study to show thyself approved unto God, a workman that need not be ashamed, rightly dividing the Word of truth" (2 Timothy 2:15 KJV). "And be not conformed to this world but be ye transformed by the renewing of your mind, That ye may prove what is that good, and acceptable, and perfect will of God" (Romans 12:2 KJV).

9. **Stay in a posture of worship.** Don't worry, you can do this and still have a life. Worship is not singing three slow Gospel or Christian songs with your hands lifted or lying prostrate on the floor all day. True worship begins in your heart, and it starts with keeping God first in your life and living a holy lifestyle. Holiness is our way of giving God our best in everything we do and say. Living a life that is pleasing to Him and walking according to His Holy will. Jesus said in John 4:23, "But the hour cometh, and now is, when the true worshippers shall worship the Father in spirit and in truth: For the Father seeketh such to worship Him. God is a spirit; and they that worship Him must worship Him in spirit and in truth."

10. **Fast and pray.** This will help you get your flesh under subjection and walk in greater discipline while building a closer and more intimate relationship with God.

True worship unto God is surrendering your will to God, loving Him more than anything and living a life of holiness that God would be glorified. Be mindful of what you allow in your spirit by the music you listen to, the things you watch on TV, and the places you go. Be diligent to surround yourself with strong believers. Avail yourself to serve as often as you can wherever you can be a blessing. Remember, idle time is the devil's workshop.

Part Two

The responsibility of holding someone accountable

1. **Make sure you can avail yourself to that person reasonably to be there when they need you to talk or be there personally.** Do not sign up for something you are not going to follow through with or take seriously. If you think you are not the person for the job, then tell them as soon as they ask you. Do not have someone thinking they can depend on you and you have no intentions of being there or you've already spread yourself so thin that you know you won't be able to render much time to them if they need you. When people are crying out and they have confided in you, they need you to be available. Otherwise, do not agree to it. Minister Claudia and Pastor Aye were two of the busiest people I know, so I was patient when I needed to be, but to be honest, they made a way to talk to me when I needed them to.

2. **Be sure to hold whatever is told to you in the strictest of confidence.** Love covers a multitude of sins (1 Peter 4:8). You are not to share with your spouse, pastor, or anyone what the person who told you didn't give you permission to tell. Some of my friends will read this book and wonder why I never confided in them. One of the reasons will be because I know you tell your spouse everything. And I wasn't comfortable with that.

3. **Make sure your own house is in order before trying to clean up someone else's mess.** If you're dealing with your own situations in life and you need to devote time to work on you, this may not be a good time to commit to helping someone else. It's noble, but not really wise.

4. **If someone ask for you to hold them accountable and you don't have a strong prayer life, either get ready to develop one or don't agree to holding them accountable.** You will need to be interceding on their behalf as often as

you can. You need to know how to pray for them and with them fervently and effectually (James 5:16).

5. **Guard your heart as well while you are holding them accountable.** Galatians 6:1: "Brothers, if someone is overtaken in a fault, you who are spiritual restore such a one in the spirit of meekness, considering thyself, lest thou also be tempted." Don't be all willy-nilly about the situation like it could never be you. Take it very serious and stay girded up in the full armor of God.

6. **Desire their restoration more than anything else from them.** This will help you keep things in perspective and stay on task. Don't get distracted by things sent by the enemy to turn your focus from getting them restored. If it gets to be too much for you and you can no longer handle it, be honest with them and let them know. But try not to be one who gives up on them easily. Sometimes it may look like they are not fighting when they really are. Ask God for discernment to know when it's a wrap.

7. **Ask the hard questions.** This is not for the faint at heart. If they came to you for accountability, they did so not expecting you to treat them like a three-year-old. They know that accountability would challenge them to be the realest they've ever been and that means bearing their souls. We ask for accountability because we want to overcome whatever we got caught up in. If someone asked for accountability and told you the ugly truth about something that they are dealing with, you can best believe they don't want to be there. And they are counting on you to help them get out. But you can't do that without pertinent information. Ask whatever questions you think you need to know that will help you understand better how they got there. I remember telling one of my goddaughters about my failures, not realizing she would take it so hard. She didn't talk to me for a minute, and when she did decide to sit down and talk to me, she was one of the ones who asked the hard questions. And although we cried together that day, I was glad she

asked the hard questions. I was glad she showed her anger for what I did without being indignant. She expected more from me and it was hard for her to hear my truth. And she didn't pretend it wasn't. I appreciated her for that. It showed me the gravity of my indiscretions. Not that I didn't know but to see the people I hurt present, past and future tense. I came to realize this would affect me for years, even with people I have yet to meet.

Chapter 20

Luke 22:32
Strengthen Your Brothers

Spiritual seduction is real though many Christians and even pastors don't believe it is. I can't say I didn't believe in it... like many Christians, I was ignorant to it. People wake up and find themselves in situations they would've never thought possible in their lives because it was something they never considered or desired. Yet all of a sudden, they are overtaken by it, and before they know it, they are kneedeep in it. And it could be anything from homosexuality to drinking, cussing, adultery, gambling, smoking, stealing, greed, etc. Just all of a sudden, you find yourself doing something you don't want to be doing. And it feels like a strong addiction. I think that's one thing that helped me because I abhor addiction to anything because I saw what it did to my family. I want nothing controlling me but the Holy Spirit. I also hate hypocrisy and I refuse to be a hypocrite. I've seen too much of that in my life, and it turned me against the church at one point in my life and I never wanted to do that to anyone else because someone is always watching you. I hate sin and I want to keep it out of my life as much as I can. Because I adore my Father and I want to live my life pleasing to Him in every way. I expected to fall short sometimes. I knew I was nowhere near perfect, but I never expected to fall that hard. And the hardest part for me was sinning in something that I had no desire for. I could not understand this for the life of me. I never thought of myself as arrogant or self-righteous, but I remember thinking highly of myself for not falling into sin. But my thought process was, "I may fall short sometimes, but at least it's not that sin, or I would never do that." And one day I found myself doing the very thing I condemned others for doing.

The funniest thing about all this is I was so self-righteous that I remember I was in the Christian bookstore in 2003 and I came across a book by Beth Moore called *When Godly People Do Ungodly Things*. I thought this had to be the dumbest book ever written! Why would anyone write such a book except to give Christians an excuse to sin? Now, I had not read one page in the book. I simply saw it and decided it was ridiculous to write such a book. I literally "judged a book by its cover." I was vexed in my spirit after coming across her book that day.

Three years later, in the fall of 2006, I would come across this book again in a bookstore at a church I decided to visit for Bible study. Only this time, I saw the book completely different. This time the title resonated with me because I was one of the godly people who had done ungodly things that year and the title of the book suggested that it could help me understand why. I was strongly compelled to buy the book even though I still hadn't read one page.

When I got the book home and began to read it, I wasn't even halfway through the first chapter before I found tears streaming down my face because she was describing exactly what had happened to me. Even to this day, should I pick up that book to refer back to something, it brings tears to my eyes. God truly used her to expose spiritual seduction by the enemy irrefutably. When this began to happen, I didn't have a clue what was really going on but I knew the enemy was behind it. I know I felt seduced because I knew what I liked and I was very experienced sexually but I'd never felt what was coming over me with this situation, so I knew it wasn't natural and I knew it wasn't me.

It was only God that led me back to that book three years later because when I saw it in 2003, I was too judgmental and self-righteous to comprehend the need for such a book, let alone open it to see what it had to offer. But now three years later, the title describes me. I strongly suggest you read it for yourself to better understand spiritual seduction. Beth Moore does an amazing job breaking the Word of God down to explain it all. It's obvious she was anointed to write the book.

One of the things that I am surprised that I still get commended for is walking away from the secular industry when I was making crazy money and doing really well. Life was great, and my star was rising fast. But one fateful night in 1998, God spoke to my heart and told me that only what I did for Him would last. Everything else was in vain. That night I decided I wanted to live my life to please God. And knowing that the money would probably change drastically and all the uncertainty ahead, I made the commitment to serve Christ and to serve Him faithfully. No turning back. And once the money dwindled down completely, the struggle was pretty constant financially. But nothing has brought me greater joy than living my life to serve my Father in heaven. I'm often baffled by the praise I (still) get for making that decision, because it would have been utterly foolish to choose otherwise. But it blesses me to know that it helped others make the same choice because I hear those testimonies all the time. I remember Pastor Aye telling me that the devil wanted to destroy my testimony. When I read the book, Beth talks about how the enemy comes after the testimonies of the saints. The more influential, the better, she says (page 12 of her book).

I was floored when I read this in her book because I immediately thought this was what Pastor Aye had said to me months before when I initially told him what I was dealing with. I wish I was truly able to express to you all how many days I sat around scratching my head trying to figure out what just happened. Why was I entertaining something I had no desire for? And why can't I just walk away. I even remember thinking that it was unfair that the enemy was able to do such a thing. Now I hated him with a passion. Now I saw the devil for how ruthless he could really be. "Be sober and vigilant because your adversary the devil, as a roaring lion, walketh about seeking whom he may devour" (1 Peter 5:8). Many of us fall prey to the enemy because we are ignorant to his schemes and devices and we don't think of how he truly wishes to devour God's children.

It is very important for us to know how cunning and crafty the devil really is. And that we always have to have on the full armor of God. Be mindful once you get past something to not let your guards down. It's okay if it has become a thorn in your flesh. "And lest I should be exalted above measure through the abundance of the revelations, there was given me a thorn in the flesh, the messenger of Satan to buffet me, lest I should be exalted above measure. For this thing I besought the Lord thrice, that it might depart from me. And He said unto me, My grace is sufficient for thee; for my strength is made perfect in weakness. Most gladly therefore, will I rather glory in my infirmities, that the power of Christ may rest upon me. Therefore, I take pleasure in infirmities, in reproaches, in necessities, in persecutions, in distresses for Christ's sake: For when I am weak, then I am strong" (2 Corinthians 12:7–10).

That's God's way of humbling us and reminding us to keep our guards up (the full armor of God) (Ephesians 6:1). That no matter what we are going through as children of the most high God, He's got us. His grace is sufficient to keep us if or when we fall, but not to be abused. The grace of God is not a license for immorality (Jude 1:4 NIV).

But we have to be mindful to love and extend that same grace to our brothers and sisters who are fighting to overcome sin. No matter how far you have gone, you are not out of God's reach. But unconfessed sin cannot be forgiven. Some people are sick in their bodies and many can't sleep at night because they have unconfessed sin in their lives that they don't want anyone to know about. Many wish they had someone they could trust to confide in, but so many in the church have betrayed people who trusted them that it's hard to get people who are suffering in silence to seek help now. When we commit ourselves to presenting our bodies as a living sacrifice, holy and pleasing unto God, that includes keeping your mouth shut when someone comes to you to confess their sins in confidence (unless someone else's life is in danger).

Jesus told Peter that the devil desires to sift you (Peter and the other apostles) as wheat. Jesus told him that He has prayed for him that he doesn't fail and that when he overcomes strengthen his brothers (and sisters in Christ). Peter basically told Jesus that he was ready for anything that came his way and was even ready to die for Christ. Jesus responded to Peter, "Before daybreak, you will have already denied me three times" (Luke 22:31–34, paraphrase).

Here we see that Jesus knows that the enemy is going to come for us, and for this reason, He sits at the right hand of the Father, making intercessions on our behalf that we don't fail. Even though He knew Peter was going to fail because He told him he would before daybreak. But He told Peter that once he had repented to go back and strengthen (enlighten, encourage, inspire) your brothers and sisters in Christ by your testimony what you have learned through your failure that they may not make the same mistakes and that they will know how to overcome as you did.

Some of us, like Peter, are so sold out to Jesus that we cannot fathom that we would ever sin against God knowing what we know of Him. Loving Him like we love Him. Having divine revelation knowledge of who He is. Yet we, like Peter, though the Lord has prayed that we don't fail, and He is more than able to keep us from falling, we find ourselves in sin, needing to repent to be forgiven.

After Jesus's resurrection, He restored Peter by allowing him to profess his love for Him three times and charging Peter to feed His sheep. Peter was now restored and given an awesome charge by the Lord Jesus to tend to that which was important to Him, His sheep (His children). But I'm willing to bet (figure of speech) that Peter was forever reminded in some way that he literally denied Christ three times even after he was told he would. Who does that? This is the same guy who walked on water with Jesus! You would've thought after the second time he would've been like "Hey, wait a minute... I know what's going on! You almost got me!" LOL!

But I'm sure this failure became a bit of a "thorn in his flesh" that kept him humble and compassionate towards others from that point on as he would be sent out to win multitudes for Christ.

And as Peter would go on to fulfill the charge that Jesus gave him, he would do so in great humility, not the usual haughty and high-minded person he was before his failure. Because now he was aware that any of us are susceptible to falling in to sin at any given time, whether you think so or not. And so we have to be careful not to condemn others when they fall without knowing their story. We have to cover one another in love, for love covers a multitude of sins (1 Peter 4:8). God has called us to love one another as He has loved us, we are to love one another. He says, "By this they will know you are my disciples, if you have love one for another" (John 13:34–35, paraphrase).

For years I loathed the thought of my incredible failure. I was angry at myself for being so weak and gullible. But when I came to realize that God would use this experience (as horrible as I thought it was) to humble me and mature me in the way of Christ, I like Paul began to embrace the "thorn in my flesh." And what the enemy meant for my harm, God would turn it around for my good. Because I'm not going to keep silent about seducing spirits and I won't be talking about what I heard... I'll be speaking on what I know. It is my prayer that my testimony will encourage everyone who has been tormented in any way by seducing spirits, whether you knew what it was or not, to be silent no more. Expose the devil for the deceiver he is, that yokes of bondage will be destroyed and obliterated, captives will be set free, broken hearts will be healed, joy will be restored, and Salvation will be received in Jesus's name. And that God would get all the glory.

I hate that I was so pigheaded that it took something so devastating to teach me humility and love according to the will of God. I thought I was doing it right, but I was doing it all wrong. Like Saul, in my zeal for God and my lack of knowledge, I was persecuting the church (with condemnation). But like Saul (turned Paul), I did it in ignorance, but once I got it, I determined in my heart that I will admit my failure and proclaim the truth of God's Word all the more and expose the enemy's schemes and tactics. I refuse to let the devil reduce me to shame for my failures and muzzle me when the grace Jesus Christ provided for me has given me a clean slate. The devil wants to keep you in bondage to sin and shame by your silence.

R. Zaccharias puts it like this, "Sin takes you farther than you wanted to go, keeps you longer than you wanted to stay and cost you more than you wanted to pay." I can attest to that.

But praise be to God that Revelations 12:11 tells us that we overcome him by the Blood of the Lamb and by the Word of our testimony; and we love not our own lives even unto death. I can absolutely attest to this truth! Thank You, Father!

And in the midst of it all, God revealed yet another truth that I try to live by daily, especially when I come across a fallen soldier on the battlefield for the Lord.

I remind myself to not be judgmental because now I know that, "but for the grace of God… there go I."

Now, how can I help them be restored?

About the Author

Chinnita Morris is a renowned Christian comedian formerly known as comedian Chocolate from HBO's *Def Comedy Jams* and BET's *ComicView*. A graduate of Winston-Salem State University, Chinnita began her comedy career shortly after graduating college. Her career took off quickly, and she thrived as a secular comedian as the fame and fortune came faster than she expected. After eight successful years of secular comedy, Chinnita surrendered her life to Christ, leaving behind a lucrative career to serve God faithfully. She is the proud mother of one daughter (Imani) and the doting grandmother of her toddler grandson (Christian).

www.ingramcontent.com/pod-product-compliance
Lightning Source LLC
Chambersburg PA
CBHW020414080526
44584CB00014B/1318